Biblical Thinking for Building Healthy Churches

info@9marks.org | www.9marks.org

Tools like this are provided by the generous investment of donors.
Each gift to 9Marks helps equip church leaders with a biblical vision and practical resources for displaying God's glory to the nations through healthy churches.

Donate at: www.9marks.org/donate.

Or make checks payable to "9Marks" and mail to:
9 Marks
525 A St. NE
Washington, DC 20002

ISBN: 9798692441898

Editorial Director: Jonathan Leeman
Editor: Sam Emadi
Managing Editor: Alex Duke
Layout: Rubner Durais
Cover Design: OpenBox9
Production Manager: Rick Denham
& Mary Beth Freeman
9Marks President: Mark Dever

CONTENTS

LEARNING FROM SCRIPTURE AND HISTORY ON PASTORING IN POLITICAL TURMOIL

PASTORING THROUGH POLITICAL TURMOIL ON SUNDAY MORNING

PASTORING IN POLITICAL TURMOIL: INTERNATIONAL PERSPECTIVES

Editor's Note:
In Praise of
Political Humility

Jonathan
Leeman

Ordinarily, the 9Marks Journals push in a theological direction. The last six issues, for instance, have covered the work of a pastor, gospel-centered preaching, complementarianism, the atonement, church membership, and Calvinism. Yet you won't be surprised to hear the number one question we're hearing from pastors these days: how do we pastor through a season of political turmoil? Hence, this issue of the Journal is devoted to pastoring through political turmoil.

Our goal is not to tell you *what* to think politically. It's to help you think about *how* to pastor when your church and country are enduring a season of political unrest or division. What posture should you adopt?

Before we jump in, let me offer a few words in praise of political humility. If politics has been characterized by pride ever since the Fall, a Christian approach to politics starts with humility, or the fear of God.

Humility in our politics means that our politics begins with the declaration, "Jesus is King." This doesn't require overturning the separation of church and state. But it does mean that a Christian's view of the state must begin with what King Jesus says about the state in his Word. A humble politics is always under God's Word, never over it.

Humility in our politics yields both courage and deference. It gives us the courage to stand fixed upon on God's Word, no matter what opposition comes. But it also teaches us to defer to others by listening to them, knowing that we can be mistaken and that our perspectives are limited.

Humility in our politics means we can learn from different kinds of people, including from people who disagree with us politically. It means we're open to critique. We don't assume all our political judgments are correct, while the other sides are all wrong, as if God showed all favor to us and none to them. That kind of tribalism

is typical in the world. It should not be typical among the saints. We know we're finite and fallen, and so we're willing to have conversations.

Humility in our politics means we show honor to everyone made in God's image, including our political opponents. We don't demonize them, but view them charitably. Just earlier today, I overheard Mark Dever say, "When we view people's political opinions in the best possible light, we're more likely than not to represent them accurately." His humility yields charity, which yields more accuracy than not. I offer the flip side of Dever's truism in my article: when we view people in the worst possible light, we're more likely than not to misrepresent them, which is a kind of dishonesty, which roots ultimately back in our pride.

Inside of a church, humility in politics works hard to distinguish whole-church matters from disputable matters. That is, it humbly submits to those issues that the whole church has determined are conditions for membership. Meanwhile, it humbly agrees to set aside our differences on disputable matters when we come to the Lord's Table with brothers and sisters in Christ, and we receive one another with joy in spite of our differences.

As much as anything, pastors, we're encouraging you to model humility in your politics, a humility that trusts and stands on God's Word more than on your own political inclinations and opinions. If you scan the Journal's table of contents, you'll see that a humble posture is the implicit goal of many of our articles.

Political humility is what's missing from the political landscape of the nations (Ps. 2:1-3). It's the principle antidote to our messes. It's the very thing which our Lord Jesus Christ demonstrated as this king made himself a servant, humbling himself to death, even death on a cross (Phil. 2:5-11). And it's what you, my beloved and politically afflicted pastor, now have the opportunity to model after our King—both in the calm political seasons but particularly in the tough ones.

13 Principles for Pastoring Through Political Turmoil

Jonathan Leeman

How can pastors lead through a tough political season?

Depending where you are, you face different challenges. Here are some real examples I've heard lately. A pastor in China is trying to figure out how to gather his church again after police broke it up and incarcerated him for two weeks.

A pastor in the Middle East wants to know what to do with members whose anti-Israel sentiments make them sympathetic to violent action against Israel.

A pastor in Northern Ireland has members who despise the British government and others who love it.

A pastor in the United States has one member calling President Trump the anti-Christ on social media, and another naming him the lion of the tribe of Judah.

We feel the political heat for different reasons, but we all feel it. How do we endure? Here are thirteen principles for pastoring through political turmoil.

1. KNOW WHAT YOU'RE UP AGAINST POLITICALLY: IDOLATRY AND FALSE WORSHIP INSIDE AND OUTSIDE THE CHURCH.

Americans tend to think we can keep our politics and our religion separate. But we can't. It's impossible. As I've written at length, our politics serve our worship. Our governments serve our gods. Political heat flows out of religious heat. Just ask Shadrach, Meshach, and Abednego. The nations will burn us when we refuse to worship their gods, whether their gods are named Bel or Marduk, money or sex, science or technology, safety or skin color, this party or that party.

Yes, God in his matchless wisdom uses those governments to restrain evil and provide peace and order (Gen. 9:5–6; 1 Tim. 2:1–4). Yes, some governments are better than others, even dramatically so (compare Pharaohs at the times of Joseph and Moses). Yet make no mistake: the nations and kings and voters of the earth rage against the Lord and against his Messiah (Ps. 2; Rev. 13:7–8). Our politics either serve Jesus Christ or our idols (see also Deut. 32:8; Ps. 82:1–2). There's no neutrality, said Augustine.

Which means, pastor, that the pressures and encroachments you feel from the so-called political sphere worsen as a nation's idols become stronger and louder. They might even be hiding inside your members' favorite ideologies (e.g. conservatism, liberalism, socialism, nationalism). When this happens, Christians will begin to tear into each other like the world.

So know what you're up against. The political battles surrounding and invading your church are profoundly spiritual. The principalities and powers aren't interested in merely getting your members to vote a certain way. They want your church's worship. So keep a level head and a sharp eye, step circumspectly, and pray hard.

2. BE MORE VIGILANT THAN EVER ABOUT CO-OPTATION BY FIGHTING FOR THE CHURCH MORE THAN ANY POLITICAL OUTCOME.

I said the principalities and powers want the church's worship. The most common way for them to do this is by co-opting us. They convince us that that the temporary kingdoms of this world are most important, their battles most crucial, their threats most to be feared, their promises most to be sought. They distract us and subvert us with good things that are not ultimate things.

From God's people in the wilderness longing to return to Egypt, to Judah's kings relying on the horses and chariots of surrounding nations, to the people of Jerusalem laying down palm branches for Jesus hoping for their rescue from Rome, to Peter picking up a sword in the Garden of Gethsemane, co-optation has always been one of the greatest threats for God's people. The world and its eyes of flesh will always want us to give its battles an outsized importance, and both sides of any battle will always clamor for our support. I assume, pastor, you've felt this from both the right and the left.

It's like two of my daughters in a squabble. Both girls want to enlist me, so that I vindicate one and denounce the other. In any given tiff, of course, I might decide one is more right than the other. Yet I serve them best by never being co-opted by either, but always being the dad, whose eye remains focused on the bigger picture for both of them. Their third and fourth sister might jump in and play favorites. I cannot do that. I have to listen to each, but the need is to be *in, not of.* If I do take sides, at most it will be temporary.

So with you, pastor. Forces outside your church will constantly try to co-opt your church to its cause. Yet often it will be your members, and you can assume they have the best of goals when they do. Their goal will be justice and righteousness, or at least justice and righteousness by their political lights. In other words, the temptation is not necessarily to something that, in and of itself, is untrue or unjust, though that happens, too. The primary temptation is to wrong priorities and the loss of an eternal, kingdom focus, which only eyes of faith can see.

When co-optation happens, without fully realizing it, you begin to prioritize nation, party, movement, election, nomination, or some other political cause over the kingdom of Christ. When co-optation happens, the volume, tone, intensity, and frequency with which you discuss political things increases. You begin to map out the world in black hats and white hats with your church wearing the white hats—as if you've forgotten what Jesus said about the plank and the speck, or what Peter said about judgment beginning with God's household. You even characterize other believers as wearing the black hats. They become the enemy. And in all of this, you tell the world that Christians are just a branch of this or that party, this or that political cause. You allow your witness to be undermined.

To be sure, politicians, parties, and the media will co-opt you even when you actively resist. A candidate might suggest the possibility of speaking at your church. A journalist will ascribe your church's action to the fact that your church is "White" or "progressive," dismissing the possibility that your church did what it did as a matter of obedience to Jesus. These things *will* happen, no matter how careful you are, because the world loves to recruit us for *its* battles. Don't help them. Don't let them enlist you. Instead, help the church to store up its treasure in heaven, not on earth.

For a moment, I want to speak specifically to Americans: we need to realize that we have a long history of co-optation. It has shown up every time American exceptionalism (and there are better and worse forms) has tempted us to confuse American history with salvation history. As goes the United States, so goes the kingdom of God. Few pastors explicitly think, "American history is salvation history." But whether we tend in a premillennial or postmillennial direction, we bear a sense of descending or ascending toward the fulfillment of all things, and of America's special place in that drama. So we place an eschatological weight on the next election, the next Court nomination, the outcome of the latest round of protests and riots. We step into the pulpit and feel burdened, not merely to fight for justice in the short-term for our neighbors, but for something a little weightier, something historical and redemptive, similar to how our post-Christian friends reveal their millennial Christian roots by talking about being on "the right side of history." As a result, our political convictions take on a holy purpose, fervor, and certitude. Preaching our historical and political judgments *becomes* preaching Scripture.

No doubt, pastors should sometimes make such historical and political judgments and call their churches to do the same. My point is not to say we must separate our politics from our religion, as the nineteenth-century doctrine of the spirituality of the church tried to do. That's the wrong solution. Politics is not separate from our biblical obedience, but one aspect of it. The point is to realize that what seems normal to pastors in the United States, whether on the left or right, may not seem normal to Christians elsewhere. Millenarianism roots deep in our national DNA, which yields a kind of utopianism, which in turn causes us to wrongly elevate both the significance and the accuracy of our historical

judgments, as if the kingdom of God depended upon them. It doesn't. Not in the slightest. No man knows the day or hour Christ will come (Matt. 24:36). Two hundred years from now the United States might look no more significant to salvation history than the kingdom of Prussia looks to us today.

Furthermore, realize how dark co-optation is. When we give more attention to the kingdoms of this world than the kingdom of Christ, we give the evil one our worship:

> Again, the devil took him to a very high mountain and showed him all the kingdoms of the world and their splendor. "All this I will give you," he said, "if you will bow down and worship me." (Matt. 4:8–9)

We must give thanks for our nations, each of us, but remind and remind and remind your congregation of their exilic status and their citizenship in heaven. Prioritize love of church—in all its colorful parts—over love of nation. Prioritize the Bible's teaching over your preferred political philosophy or partisan leanings, even when you're convinced those leanings are correct. Satan loves to sidetrack Christian pastors with their political certitudes. Continue to love and embrace a church member whose political opinions frustrate you, assuming those opinions or activities do not put him or her under the discipline of the church.

3. TRUST THE POINT OF WHATEVER BIBLE BOOK YOU'RE PREACHING THROUGH RIGHT NOW.

You and your church will be able to follow principles 1 and 2 only as Scripture shapes you (see Rom. 12:2). The concerns of your Twitter feed shouldn't dictate what they're learning. The Bible should.

So keep preaching consecutively through books of the Bible. Are you preaching Mark 1 this week? Then the point of Mark 1 is what your people most need. Mark 2? Then they most need the point of Mark 2. Mark 3? You see where I'm going.

Pastors love that quote about preaching with the Bible in one hand and the newspaper in the other. Fine, but I hope you're a whole lot more confident in your judgments and exposition of Scripture than you are in your exposition of the significance of events in your newspaper. Don't treat your two hands symmetrically.

I'm not saying you don't ever offer topical sermons on pertinent questions. I am saying the long-term, culture-shaping project of helping your church to endure tough political seasons depends on your long-term commitment to expositional preaching. The Holy Spirit revealed Mark 1, 2 and 3 for a reason. There's something in them your church *needs*.

Oliver O'Donovan helps us to transition from the last two principles to this one when he says,

Not every wave of political enthusiasm deserves the attention of the church in its liturgy. Judging when political questions merit prophetic commentary requires a cool head and a theological sense of priorities. The worship that the principalities and powers seek to extract from mankind is a kind of feverish excitement. The first business of the church is to refuse them that worship. There are many times—and surely a major election is one of them—when the most pointed political criticism imaginable is to talk about something else.

And that something else, most critically, is the Bible.

More inspired than O'Donovan is the apostle Paul. Paul points us to the Bible as the weapons we use to demolish the strongholds that are set up against the knowledge of God.

The weapons we fight with are not the weapons of the world. On the contrary, they have divine power to demolish strongholds. We demolish arguments and every pretension that sets itself up against the knowledge of God, and we take captive every thought to make it obedient to Christ. (2 Cor. 10:4–5)

The louder the idols become and the more political heat we feel, the more crucial it is for you to preach the Bible expositionally, letting God set the agenda, not the gods.

4. BE A DRAMA DAMPENER, NOT AN ACCELERATOR.

People love drama, political and otherwise, and one of your jobs, pastor, is to tamp it down when it divides the saints or distracts them from matters of first importance. Model peacemaking (Matt. 5:9) because not every disagreement needs to turn into a heresy trial. Remind your members that they're family; they've agreed to unite around repentance from sin and your statement of faith, not their political judgments.

Also, check your own heart: do you love drama? So does Satan. He rejoices when he provokes the saints to gasp and whisper about one another, "I can't believe he…?!" or "If that law passes the world will end!" Therefore, the best pastors (and parents!) I know are drama dampeners, not accelerators. They teach members how to give one another the benefit of the doubt amidst the tiffs and kerfuffles.

Being a drama dampener is tough if you love to brawl. Confess and repent if you do. Also, the so-called discernment bloggers and YouTubers thrive on drama and division. Avoid them, and tell your members to do the same. Certainly be careful about your own presence on social media (here are five observations and four tips for pastors engaging on social media).

I admit I've never lived in a war-torn nation, under the threat of persecution by a secular dictator or Muslim radicals, or as an oppressed minority. I trust my perspective would shift some in each. Yet even in all of these circumstances, there are those who love drama and those who dampen it, because they trust in God. Your goal and mine should be to model peacemaking and mature conversation. Related to that . . .

5. BECOME AN EXPERT IN FEAR AND HOPE.

The purpose of politics is to pursue justice, which is good. But politics in this world is driven by fear, which is at best mixed. Fear of destruction and harm. Fear of the bad guys winning and my side losing. Fear of injustice. Fear is the common currency.

In politically tumultuous times, fear runs rampant, and people act like cornered dogs who growl and snarl. They also flee to the populist voices that speak with certainty and confidence, assuring their listeners that they wear the white hats while everyone else wears a black hat.

Your job, pastor, is to respond by playing part shepherd, part prophet, and part ambassador for the king who knows no fear but offers hope.

The shepherd in you must acknowledge that some of these enemies—the existential threats that comprise the political landscape—are real. A shepherd doesn't say, "There are no wolves and enemies." Rather, he prepares a table for his congregation in the presence of their enemies (Ps. 23:5). He points them to the quiet waters of Christ's love and the green pastures of his Word, even as very real enemies surround us (see also Ps. 3:6).

The prophet in you, however, reminds your church that there is something we should fear more than the existential threats posed by this world, and that's the eternal threat of the one who holds the kings of the earth in derision and will smite them with a rod of iron (Ps. 2:4, 9). Fear God, not man. God told Isaiah to do this even as the Assyrian army loomed menacingly over Judah:

> Do not call conspiracy all that this people calls conspiracy, and do not fear what they fear, nor be in dread. But the Lord of hosts, him you shall honor as holy. Let him be your fear, and let him be your dread. (Is. 8:12–13)

Christian writers often emphasize the church's "prophetic" role in calling out the sins of a nation. Yet notice: for every chapter the biblical prophets devote to indicting the nations, they devote several to indicting God's own people. Which is to say, the primary role of prophesy among God's people is self-indictment, not others-indictment. Judgment begins with the household of God (see Matt. 7:3–5; 1 Pet. 4:17).

So, pastor, do you spend more time calling out the evils of political forces "out there," or more time helping your church to discern their own misplaced fears? One of the main lessons of the whole Old Testament was that Israel's greatest enemy was never Egypt, the Philistines, Assyria, or Babylon. It was always their own hearts. Maybe we should spend less time being culture warriors and more time being gospel proclaimers?

The ambassador in you, then, reminds your church that they're citizens of another city whose architect and builder is God (Phil. 3:20; Heb. 11:10). The fear and panic they feel too often roots in the fact that they think this world really is their home and they're expecting something more (see point 2 above). We shouldn't be surprised when pedophilia goes mainstream on Netflix or when police officers in my county throw a man to the ground during a traffic stop and leave him partially paralyzed. This sounds a lot like the Roman Empire of Jesus' and Paul's day, doesn't it? The point isn't to speak against such evil less, but to remind them of eternity more.

Yet the most crucial step in all of this, pastor is for you not to live submerged in fear. One drowning man isn't much help to another.

The solution to fear is hope. Do your sermons usually end in hope?

Something that's common amidst political turmoil is to view those who disagree with us darkly and cynically. When we view people in the worst possible light, we tend to misrepresent them. And to misrepresent someone is to be dishonest. We may not *mean* to deceive, but the combination of our cynicism and carelessness begets this dishonesty, for which we are culpable.

We become so convinced of the justice of our cause that we begin to believe *our assumptions* about the other side as much as *what the other side actually said*. So we exaggerate. We impugn motives. We insist people believe things they explicitly deny. We attack *them* and not just *what they're saying*. We call our family unity into question, saying things like, "I can't believe how much you've moved from where you used to be!" Such a charge might be appropriate a couple times a decade, but not once a week.

Remember who Psalm 15:3 says can live on the Lord's holy mountain: the one who does not "discredit his neighbor" (CSB).

How many times have I been tempted to discredit a fellow believer who is making different political judgments than my own? It's easy to do, whether in a text message to a friend or publicly on Twitter. Yet the solution is simple: leave judgment to the Lord and give fellow believers the benefit of the doubt.

And model this for your church. When a member whispers to you, "Can you believe he...?!" offer a more charitable, "Well, is it possible he actually...?"

7. DECLARE THE STANDARDS BY WHICH THE NATIONS WILL BE JUDGED.

The last several points must be coupled with this point because, amidst charity, we must draw lines, too. I borrow the language here from a 1967 article by Carl F. H. Henry. He said the church's job is "to declare the criteria by which nations will ultimately be judged, and the divine standards to which man and society must conform if civilization is to endure."

Part of fearing God is knowing that God will judge all nations—"the kings of the earth and the great ones and the generals and the rich and the powerful, and everyone, slave and free" (Rev. 6:15). Your job, pastor, is to help both your members and any visitors know what the biblical criteria of judgment will be. You do this to warn and instruct your church for the purposes of their political engagement. You also do it to lovingly warn the outsider.

To do this well you need a good biblical theology and a good biblical theology of government. You should be able to answer questions like:

- What has God authorized the governments of all nations to do? What is their jurisdiction?
- Peter says the task of government is "to punish those who do evil and praise those who do good" (1 Pet. 2:14). Is he referring to every conceivable evil and good, or a subset of them? In other words, do we criminalize all sin or certain sins?
- What is justice in the Bible?
- Do we regard the civil commands and episodes in the life of Old Covenant Israel as directly binding on the church or as illustrative?
- Is religious liberty biblical? What is it?
- Which kinds of political judgments bind the whole church, and which can be left in the category of Christian freedom?
- What's the relationship between church and state?

Indeed, I've been on my own 15-year-long quest to carve out a more biblical political theology in order to answer such questions. But you need to study the Scriptures for yourself. Then declare what the Bible says justice is and the criteria by which the nations and their governments will be judged. God's judgment later means he rules the earth now, whether people acknowledge him or not: "Say among the nations, 'The Lord reigns! . . . he will judge the peoples with equity'" (Ps. 96:10).

8. BEWARE A BURGEONING FUNDAMENTALISM AND AUTHORITARIANISM.

Political science 101 will teach you that authoritarian leaders and philosophies become increasingly viable in seasons of political opposition or turmoil. When our values, freedoms, and lives feel threatened, the authoritarian philosophy and leader looks reassuring. He offers security. One economist has observed that authoritarianism isn't synonymous with any one ideological framework, but "is a functional disposition concerned with maximizing 'oneness' and 'sameness' especially in conditions where the things that make us one and the same—common authority, and shared values—appear to be under threat."

Furthermore, authoritarian leaders cultivate or are accompanied by fundamentalistic cultures, in the pejorative sense of that term. When the political and cultural stakes feel too high, we give up on the "right to be wrong" in the public square (see Jonah Goldberg's article on this topic here) as well as Christian liberty in the church.

In a fundamentalistic culture, members and leaders both give themselves to policing language. They become preoccupied with doctrinal purity tests and treat everything as of first importance. They fashion new rules. They insist on subscription to their own initiatives as a test of solidarity and faithfulness. They countenance little self-critique among tribe members. And they quickly denounce the slightest infractions for party infidelity.

The popular imagination often identifies these tendencies with the political and theological right. For instance, it's easy to recount the surge toward fundamentalism among some conservative Christian churches in the first half of the twentieth-century in response to the growing acceptance of Darwinian scientific naturalism in Western culture. Yet the "functional disposition" of a fundamentalism and authoritarianism settles into leftward trajectories as easily as rightward ones.

Sure enough, resurgent iterations of old and discarded authoritarian theories of government have regained currency of late on both the political right and left. Christians on the right cast hungry glances both at Roman Catholic integralism and Old Covenant theonomy. Christians on the left meanwhile tilt at least one ear toward the neo-Marxist strains of critical theory. Both sides go tit for tat, fighting fire with fire, each accusing the other of authoritarianism while cultivating its own, when what's really needed from the church is the water of the gospel. The

gospel, after all, necessitates more space for Christian freedom (see next point).

Another possible blind-spot of my own side—the right—is our taste over the last 60 or 70 years for conference-stage apologists, evangelists, and pastors who don't just declare the Bible boldly, but who adopt a tone of certainty no matter what they were talking about, who dismiss secular opponents with a clever quip, who do what today's called "owning the libs," and who default to tropes instead of discussion and judgments instead of reconciliation. The more tumultuous our political environment becomes, the more that posture will seem attractive. Think of how popular Donald Trump's bravado is among his supporters.

No doubt, strong leadership is often necessary in the face of opposition and turmoil. When the civic order shakes, everyone wants stability. When confusion reigns, we need someone to say, "Walk this way." Yet good and bad guys alike emerge in such seasons, and our job as pastors is to keep our eyes peeled for a resurgence of fundamentalism and authoritarianism in the church, including in ourselves. Several decades of Christian books, radio programs, and social media feeds endlessly recounting stories of cultural declension have helped lay a fertile seedbed for such a resurgence. After each radio program, we wonder, is the sky falling?

So be careful. Don't get distracted. Remain as fixed and confident of the Bible as ever, holding firmly to the trustworthy message as its been taught (Titus 1:9). People's itching ears will insist you say more. But you must preach the Word with great patience (2 Tim. 4:2–3).

Maintain a good sense of theological triage. Ask your wife and fellow elders if you tend to live in a defensive, protective posture, not a risk-taking, hope-giving, evangelistic one. And don't confuse strength with displays of strength. True strength is "humble and contrite in spirit and trembles at [God's] word" (Isa. 66:2). It constantly listens for correction, even when you're the top dog, because you know the task is always to "work out your salvation with fear and trembling" (Phil. 2:12). True strength remains obedient to the exhortation, "today, if you hear his voice, do not harden your hearts" (Heb. 4:7).

9. BE THE BIGGEST ADVOCATE OF CHRISTIAN FREEDOM IN YOUR CHURCH.

Another crucial way to work against a legalistic fundamentalism and authoritarianism in your preaching and leadership—if that's a risk for you—is to work at being the biggest advocate of Christian freedom in your church.

To be sure, it's a challenge to find that line between discipling people to think biblically in their politics and wrongly binding their consciences. Yet we don't want to mimic the Pharisees who added to God's law, heaping up burdens all in the name of playing it safe. Your job is to teach the congregation how to "welcome one another" in disputable matters, and not to "pass judgment" on each other in matters of conscience (Rom. 14:1, 3, 4, 10).

Part of being an advocate for Christian freedom is helping your church to recognize the distinction between straight-line judgments and jagged-line judgments. Straight-line judgments offer a "straight line" between a theological or ethical principle found in the Bible and a political conviction. For instance, the Bible says everyone is made in God's image, even from the womb, and we might say there's a relatively straight line in moving from those biblical texts to a prohibition against abortion. Therefore, pastor, you can speak in a conscience-binding way.

Meanwhile, jagged-line judgments might begin with biblical principles, but one has to take a jagged path to arrive at policy solutions. Suppose a Christian wants to argue for universal health care as a human right. He might start with an ethical claim about human rights as a biblical idea, but from there the argument has to move back and forth down a jagged path, satisfactorily answering multiple questions on which Christians might reasonably disagree: What services would be covered? At what cost to the taxpayers? What would the economic trade-offs be, and are those just? What if standards of care dramatically drop, such that more people cannot receive life-saving treatment?

As we're trying to divide straight-line and jagged-line judgments, we need to recognize that there's an ethical asymmetry between "musts" and "must nots." It's easier to apply the authority of the Bible in saying something like, "You must not marry Joe because he's a non-Christian," than to say, "You must marry Jim, who is a Christian." By the same token, there's a lower ethical bar to *proscribing* particular political paths ("Christians must not support abortion") than there is to *prescribing* particular paths ("Christians must protest this Saturday at the march"). We more quickly step beyond our authority as pastors when we tell them precisely how to fulfill certain biblical duties—when we tell them which strategies or tactics to adopt.

In general, we should teach our congregation how to have healthy, mature discussions in jagged-line matters, even to work to persuade each other. Yet in such matters we're to help them make sure they don't make their position *the* standard of Christian righteousness and faithfulness.

Modeling and teaching your church Christian liberty amidst political tumult is crucial for at least three reasons.

First, it preserves the church and its unity by lowering the temperature in our political conversations. Mind you, the call to unity doesn't mean Christians can never disagree with one another, even publicly. We don't want a false and shallow unity. Nonetheless, the call to unity does mean that, when we disagree, we try to do so charitably, giving one another the benefit of the doubt, and affirming our ongoing gospel partnership, assuming this is possible.

Second, advocating for Christian freedom affirms the unique authority of the Bible and builds our unity on the Bible. We protect the unique authority of Scripture by insisting on the distinction between straight-line and jagged-line judgments.

Third, advocating for Christian freedom protects the gospel. A consistent and unchecked disregard for the Christian freedom of other saints and churches will create a culture of legalism. And legalism effectively undermines the gospel, even if it's unintentional. Therefore, to fight for Christian freedom is to fight for the gospel, because doing so is one way we draw a line between the gospel and everything else.

Your members might want to make a case for or against racial reparations, or an immigration policy, or the timing of civil disobedience, or a hundred other things. Fine. Just make sure they continue welcoming each other to the Lord's Table amidst those different jagged-line judgments.

10. RECOGNIZE THE LIMITS OF CHRISTIAN FREEDOM.

Any full-throated affirmation of Christian freedom should acknowledge its dangers. For starters, such talk can feel like a wet blanket in a politically tumultuous season. It will dampen political rallies and campaign speeches. It tempers and moderates, which makes it difficult to lead a political charge, even when they're necessary.

More crucially, the risk of championing a Romans 14 freedom is an undiscerning compromise. It's letting gospel-compromisers into the castle, calling them "friends" when they aren't actually friends. And it risks failing to take a prophetic stand for truth or justice when we should.

It's possible that we will call something a matter of freedom that is not, even as we warn others not to make something a test of faithfulness that is actually a matter of freedom. In other words, you don't want to be the pastor who tried to rally the saints in the name of "Christian freedom" in 1859 America or 1939 Germany.

Knowing when to bind the consciences of members in political matters takes profound wisdom. Is that black and white or is that gray? Folks further to the left or the right on the political bell curve will be quicker to call matters black or white, while folks in the middle will be quicker to see gray. It's good to know yourself and your temperamental tendencies. We all have them.

But you don't want to call the grays black and white or the black and whites gray. There are times to say "Freedom" and there are times to say, "Church, we must walk this way!" Pray the Lord would give you wisdom and courage for both kinds of occasion.

11. EQUIP THE SAINTS FOR WORKS OF JUSTICE; IN OTHER WORDS, DISCIPLE THEM POLITICALLY.

Your job, pastor, is not to be a politician or pundit. It's not to prescribe political tactics or strategies. Ordinarily, it's not to tell your members how to vote (though you might give them principles for voting. See here and here). The mission of the church as an institutional, corporate actor is not to lobby, to campaign, or to pursue legislative programs. It's to make disciples (Matt. 28:18-20)

That said . . .

Your job as a pastor is also to teach your church everything Christ commanded (v. 19), which includes loving neighbor and seeking justice (Prov. 29:4; Is. 1:17; Matt. 22:39; 2 Cor. 7:11).

Christians will disagree over what justice is and what it requires. Fine. Your job is still to study the Scriptures and equip the church to seek justice—whatever your biblical studies lead you to believe it is.

Our politics are not separate from our religion. It's one aspect of our obedience. The guys who say, "Don't preach politics, preach the gospel," are half right. They're right to say you shouldn't preach a party, a strategy, or a legislative agenda, as I said a moment ago. Yet you should preach repentance and obedience. And when a people's politics involve injustice, they must repent as a part of their gospel obedience. To be sure, it takes great wisdom to know when this is the case, including the distinction between straight- and jagged-line issues described in principle 9 above.

Yet make no mistake: justified people love justice. In a virtuous cycle, our justification creates a desire for justice, which in turn displays and demonstrates our justification; just like our faith creates good deeds, which in turn display and demonstrate our faith.

Insofar as politics belongs under the umbrella of obedience, it's part of your job to disciple a congregation in how to live and think politically. Go back to the bullet points listed in principle 7 above. You want to equip your congregation with answers to those kinds of questions. For instance, they'll better know how to vote when they understand what God has established governments to do, and what justice requires.

The mission of the church as a corporate actor is to *make* disciples, but the mission of the church as its individual members is to *be disciples.* Your job, then, is to teach them how to be disciples who love their neighbors and seek justice. In addition to many good books on these topics, see the small group study guide here as well as a Sunday School class here.

12. GIVE HONOR TO WHOM HONOR IS DUE.

I once heard a preacher take 15 seconds to say, "Of course, we embrace Romans 13," followed by five minutes of mocking the government. Apparently he missed the last verse in the paragraph: "Pay to all what is owed to them . . . respect to whom respect is owed, honor to whom honor is owed" (Rom. 13:7). Peter, too: "Honor the emperor" (1 Peter 2:17). And it's worth recalling what kinds of emperors the apostles were talking about—not Christian-loving ones.

Or we might go back to Daniel emerging from the lions' den, standing before King Darius, and saying, "Oh, King, live forever." How could he show that pagan king such honor? Had he sold out? Daniel knew, first, that God has established Darius in his throne, so that honoring Darius was honoring God. And second, he knew that God laughs at any king who seeks to compete with him (see Ps. 2:4). God's eternal threat was far greater than Darius' existential threat, and so Daniel felt free to honor him.

The world may oppose us more than ever, but we know the end of history, which is the only thing which puts us on the right side of history. We know that Jesus wins. Therefore, alarmism, panic, and brawling do not become us. Gentleness, love, happy confidence, strength, and courage do.

13. EXPECT POLITICALLY FRUSTRATED MEMBERS TO FIND OTHER CHURCHES, AND BLESS THEM WHEN THEY GO.

It's comparatively easy to build an all-politically-conservative church or an all-progressive church. You know what red-meat words you can throw either to Baby Boomer conservatives or to Millennial progressives which communicate, "You're safe here. I see the world like you see the world." By the same token, you know what words will "trigger" and turn them off. In tough seasons, the temptation to play to one side or the other only grows. Don't. Work to build a church that's united on the truth of Scripture.

Doing this will turn some off. Members on the right and left will criticize you for both what you say and what you don't say. When they approach you in the hallway afterward, explain why you did what you did, but don't argue with them.

Affirm them where you can. Whether or not you're a one-issue voter when you step into the ballot box, you should be a multi-issue sympathizer. Why? Because God cares about multiple issues, even if some are more significant than others.

If a member's finely-tuned convictions continue to be a stumbling block for them in your church, don't panic. Tell them you understand, express your love for them, and ask if they've thought about which other churches might be better suited to their perspectives. If it's a gospel-preaching church, encourage them and bless them as they go, reminding them they're always welcome back. Maybe they'll prosper better under the teaching of God's Word in that other church without the constant provocation of your own judgments. Unless there's clear sin involved, don't let their political differences and even possible departure become a big stink. Love and forbear, even if they're conducting themselves immaturely.

Finally, make sure you're preparing your fellow elders for the possibility of such departures. It helps them not to panic when they come, and protects them from bending and making compromises they shouldn't.

Here's one last thing to say about pastoring in a politically tumultuous season: you need to assume you'll make the wrong judgments sometimes. If there's a time to build up and a time to tear down (Eccl. 3), you and I lack the wisdom to always figure out what time it is. The good news is, God never misreads the time. He knows exactly what he's doing at every moment, and we can trust in him, even when we get it wrong.

FOOTNOTES:

[1] Quoted in John D. Wilsey, *American Exceptionalism and Civil Religion: Reassessing the History of an Idea,* 56.

[2] Jacob Cushing, "Divine Judgments Upon Tyrants," in *Political Sermons of the American Founding Era: 1730-1805,* edited by Ellis Sandoz (Indianapolis: Liberty Fund, 1991), 622.

[3] There are good lessons to learn from Israel's history, no doubt. Yet we must always bear in mind that ancient Israel, whether slave or free, finds its fulfillment not in America or any subset of America, but in Christ and—by virtue of our union with him—the church. Moses is neither George Washington nor Martin Luther King, Jr.

ABOUT THE AUTHOR

Jonathan Leeman is the Editorial Director at 9Marks

Don't Get *Left Behind:*

WHY PASTORS SHOULD CONSIDER PREACHING
THROUGH REVELATION IN OUR CULTURAL MOMENT

Sam Emadi

If you want to pastor faithfully in the midst of cultural and political turmoil, then consider teaching through the book of Revelation.

Modern evangelicals tend to have an allergic response any time someone brings up Revelation's significance for "the times we live in." Don't worry. I'm not about to suggest that the COVID-19 pandemic is a fulfillment of biblical prophecy, that a particular politician is the harlot of Babylon, or that the locusts of Revelation 9 are really Apache helicopters. I didn't grow up reading *Left Behind*, but I've seen my share of "biblical" apocalypse movies. I'm not interested in following those sensationalized readings of Revelation.

If you've got a newspaper in one hand and Revelation in the other, you're probably seeing things in Scripture that simply aren't there. Revelation isn't a play-by-play of 21st century American politics. In short, if you want Revelation to inform your understanding of our culture's crises, don't get *Left Behind.*

At the same time, modern evangelicals can learn something from previous generations' preoccupation with apocalyptic literature. After all, God gave us Revelation to challenge our temporally-obsessed, earthly perspective of the world. It lifts our eyes beyond political powers, pandemics, elections, and economic crises to spiritual realities: principalities, powers, and the Christ who rules over heaven and earth. It confronts our preoccupation with the immediate and reminds us that the most important and defining features of our world are *unseen.* By diagnosing our primary problem as outside *this* realm, Revelation also reminds us that our ultimate hope lies in someone who can overcome the spiritual powers that lie behind this world's brokenness and corruption. In times of political and cultural turmoil, we need Revelation.

INTERPRETING REVELATION

At the same time, we shouldn't let sensationalized and fantastic interpretations of Revelation keep us from asking what the book has to teach us. This Journal is all about pastoring in political turmoil—and Revelation, by-and-large, is about how Christians can walk faithfully amid the world's political, cultural, and economic tumult. Every interpretive approach to Revelation ought to affirm this. Whether you're pre-, post-, or amillennial, Revelation simply *is* about disease, bloodshed, political corruption, materialism, false doctrine, war, and—let's not forget—the Christ who one day will conquer them all.

Before unpacking a few lessons Revelation can teach us about our current political moment, let me explain how I approach the book. At the risk of oversimplifying and ignoring potential "But what about...." moments you'll likely experience in the rest of this article,

I'll be brief. Revelation is a book of symbols. As Vern Poythress says, "Revelation is a picture book, not a puzzle book."[1] As we read, our first aim shouldn't be to find out what every obscure detail means but simply to look for each symbol's big idea. Again, as Poythress notes, those big ideas are pretty clear, "Praise the Lord. Cheer for the saints. Detest the Beast. Long for the final victory" (13).

The larger question, of course, is where we locate these symbols in redemptive history. Is Revelation largely a book about future events, even from our own historical location? Or do these symbols represent events throughout the history of the church, or as others assert, events surrounding the destruction of Jerusalem in AD 70?

I think, instead of identifying each symbol with a specific historical event (whether past or future) we should read these symbols *typologically*; they represent the *types* of events that recur throughout history. In other words, Revelation provides a symbolic description of the world in every culture and in every age. If 2020's pandemic, civil unrest, political decadence, government corruption, and overall tumult has felt a tad apocalyptic, well, that's because it is. These are the characteristics of a demonically influenced old-world order—one both raging against and running scared from David's heir.

I'm not denying that Revelation lays out prophetic expectations. It surely does. But even when Revelation describes events just prior to the return of Christ, those events are often the culmination of repeated patterns throughout history. Or as John might say, "As you have heard that antichrist is coming, so now many antichrists have come" (1 Jn. 2:18).[2] There's a reason every era of human history is dominated by antichrists, false teachers, wars, bloodshed, pestilence, famine, and bloodthirsty political powers. These are patterns that anticipate the final day of God's judgment, typological warnings in real, time-and-space history that reveal the coming wrath of the Lamb.

PORTRAITS OF POLITICS, POWER, AND PLEASURE IN REVELATION

So what does Revelation say about Christian faithfulness in political and cultural turmoil? Well, far more than we can cover in this article, but here's a brief summary of at least some of the data.

For the sake of simplicity, consider Revelation as consisting of two parts. Part One focuses generally on the recurring patterns of political, economic, and social turmoil that come from the Messiah's hand into our world as a sign of his coming judgment. Part Two focuses on the world powers employed by Satan to persecute and corrupt the church.

Part One begins with John's vision of the exalted Christ (Rev. 4–5)—the beating heart of Revelation's message. Here he is both the Lion of Judah and the Lamb standing as though slain. Christ's singular ability to open the scroll of heaven and break its seven seals reveals that he is the Lord of history—sovereign over political movements, military conquests, and even global pandemics. By and large, the seals,

---

1 Vern Poythress, *The Returning King* (Phillipsburg, NJ: P&R, 2000), 13. Throughout this article I have liberally relied on Vern Poythress's *The Returning King* and Dennis Johnson's *The Triumph of the Lamb* (Phillipsburg, NJ: P&R, 2001). My hope is that these quotations will whet your appetite to read these books yourselves. Poythress and Johnson write from an amillenial perspective. For an excellent premillennial commentary on Revelation, see Jim Hamilton's *Revelation: The Spirit Speaks to the Churches* (Wheation, IL: Crossway, 2012).

2 For those familiar with the terminology, I am an amillenialist and a modified idealist, one that embraces some preterist and futurist elements of Revelation. Dennis Johnson helpfully explains how modified idealism embraces the prophetic, futurist elements of Revelation: "Occasionally idealist interpreters, overreacting (I think) to futurism's fixation on the final tribulation, minimize Revelation's clear expectation that Christ's return will be preceded by a period of brief but intense persecution for the church. Revelation shows in various ways that the church's present experience of persecution, although genuinely painful, is nevertheless limited by God's powerful restraint of the dragon and. His minions. The two witnesses' enemies cannot destroy them until their testifying mission is complete, at which time the beast will conquer and kill them. The evil trio will deceive and gather the kings and nations to wage war against the Lamb and his army, the camp of the saints—but not until the dragon is released to resume the deceptive power he wielded over the Gentiles prior to Christ's death and resurrection. Idealism that pays careful attention (as we should) to all that Revelation reveals will not conclude that history will go on normally and then Jesus will return. Revelation presents a more complex picture: the kingdom is advancing and gathering in the nations through the church's witness amid suffering; and then, just before the end, intensified and coordinated hostility of the non-Christian world against the church, which is rescued by the glorious return of Jesus our Defender" (Johnson, *Triumph of the Lamb*, 363).

and the horsemen that come from them, represent the Lamb's wrath against his enemies, a provisional judgment that he will one day pour out on them without restraint. What are these judgments? Military conquests (6:1–2); war (6:3–4); scarcity and famine (6:5–6); and violence, pestilence, and death (6:7–8).

Yet through all these judgments the Lord cares for his people, keeping them for himself and promising them final deliverance (7:1–17). These provisional judgments are described again with the blasting of seven trumpets—anticipatory signs of the Lamb's wrath that echo the Egyptian plagues. The exodus allusion cements the point of these trumpet blasts. The Lord has brought political superpowers to their knees before and he will continue to do so until he comes again. He will expose the highest achievements of human ingenuity as mere pretense.

Part Two introduces the dragon (Satan) and his violent efforts to destroy Israel and ultimately the Messiah (Rev. 12:1–6). But his efforts prove vain. Having been defeated by Christ's death and resurrection, he is no longer able to access heaven and accuse the saints (12:7–11). Defeated on that front, the dragon turns his bloodlust against Christ's church on earth (12:12), empowering an unholy trinity bent on destroying Christ's people: the Beast, the false prophet, and the harlot of Babylon.

John describes the Beast as a composite of the world empires of Daniel 7: Babylon, Medo-Persia, Greece, and Rome. The Beast is an archetype of the kingdoms of the world, characterized by violence and bloodlust like the violent beasts who symbolize them. Even more striking, however, is the way the Beast attempts to assert itself as the true messiah. It presents itself as having risen from the dead (13:3), invites worship (13:4), and claims authority "over every tribe and people and language and nation" (13:7; cf. 7:9).

The false prophet primarily symbolizes false ideology and deception, particularly deception that serves the ultimate supremacy of the state (Rev. 13:14). This prophet speaks words "like a dragon"—showing it's ultimately empowered by the father of lies himself. As Poythress notes, the false prophet is the Beast's "propagandist."[3] Just as the Beast is a false messiah, the false prophet is a counterfeit Holy Spirit, testifying to the power and authority of the Beast. The false prophet bucks no rivals to the Beast, marking all who are loyal to it (13:16) and stripping those who won't bow to the Beast of their ability to buy and sell (13:17)—an attempt to impoverish the saints who won't embrace his Satanic agenda.

Finally, the harlot of Babylon represents the material and sexual seductions of the world (17:2). Like the Beast and the false prophet, she is a counterfeit—a whorish, satanic substitute of the pure bride of Christ. She allures the world into allegiance with the Beast with promises of pleasure—a pleasure that can only be realized by silencing the witness of the saints (17:6).

The rest of Revelation returns to that glorious picture of Christ in heaven. In its final chapters, we see Christ not opening the seals of prospective judgment but coming to rescue his people, fully and finally, by destroying the harlot, the false prophet, the Beast, and eventually the dragon himself.

Summing up, Revelation shows us a portrait of the world characterized by political, social, and economic turmoil. It provides us a symbolic vocabulary for seeing our world from Christ's heavenly perspective.

How then do we shepherd people in light of this? Here are five lessons Revelation teaches us in the mist of political turmoil.

FIVE LESSONS ON PASTORING IN POLITICAL TURMOIL FROM REVELATION

1. Embrace Revelation's supernatural perspective on reality.

One of the most important lessons Revelation can teach us is that things aren't always as they seem. Dennis Johnson summarizes it well:

> The church in Smyrna appears poor but is rich, and it is opposed by those who claim to be Jews but are Satan's synagogue

---

3 Poythress, 143.

(Rev. 2:9). Sardis has a reputation for life but is dead (3:1). Laodicea thinks itself rich and self-sufficient, but this church is destitute and naked (3:17). The beast seems invincible, able to conquer the saints by slaying them (11:7; 13:7); their faithfulness even to death, however, proves to be their victory over the dragon that empowered the beast (12:11). What appears to the naked eye, on the plane of human history, to be weak, helpless, hunted, poor, defeated congregations of Jesus' faithful servants prove to be the true overcomers who participate in the triumph of the Lion who conquered as a slain Lamb. What appear to be the invincible forces controlling history—the military-political religious-economic complex that is Rome and its less lustrous successors—is a system sown with the seeds of its self destruction, already feeling the first lashes of the wrath of the Lamb. On the plane of visible history things are not what they appear, so Revelation's symbols make things appear as they are."[4]

Christians should beware the hyper-naturalist pressures of our secular age. After all, if we believe the Bible, then we should shamelessly remember that we live in a world where angels are dispatched to answer the prayers of the saints but have to call in reinforcements against demonic

opposition just to reach them (Dan. 10:10–14). The world wants to make you feel silly for saying things like that. After all, if Christians get embarrassed about their supernaturalism, then it won't be long before they stop talking about a Jewish carpenter who rose from the dead.

Revelation teaches us not to succumb to the parochial, naïve interpretation this world offers of itself. Despite appearances, the powers of this world are not ultimate, the judgements of its political leaders are not final, and its pleasures are not as lasting as Satan might have us believe. The world's seductions are Satan's ruse. Despite the false prophet's propaganda, the Beast cannot save us and is not worthy of our worship. The perceived power and glamor of our political, economic, and cultural institutions will one day be revealed for what they truly are: powerless and empty.

Christians should never see the world by the standards of this age. We have access to Christ's heavenly perspective, a view of what's *truly true* and *really real*—spiritual realities behind earthly experiences. What may seem ultimate and all-consuming to the world is, in reality, a passing thing, and Christians shouldn't be taken in by the lie.

No, the next election isn't the most important political moment in history. No, the hopes of economic prosperity shouldn't dictate our every decision. No, the church isn't an irrelevant

band of defeated losers. No, it's not silly to resist illicit, worldly pleasure. No, our political parties and leaders aren't worthy of the unquestioning devotion they demand. No, resisting LGBT indoctrination is not placing yourself on "the wrong side of history."

Revelation helps us see past the façade of this world's power and glory and reminds us that at the center of creation and the fulcrum of history lies another paradox: a lion, standing as though slain (Rev. 4–5).

2. Don't be surprised by the turmoil or forget the one behind it.

Revelation reminds us that our current political and cultural upheavals are nothing out of the ordinary. The seals and trumpet blasts repeat in every generation and culture. Just consider the last century. Ten out of the 100 years were spent with the entire world at war; over 100 million people were killed as a result. In fact, humanity became so skilled at killing one another, they ignited an arms race and built weapons capable of incinerating millions at a moment's notice. In 1918, the Spanish Flu swept across the globe killing somewhere between 17–50 million people. A global depression destroyed lives and made food and resources scarce.

Moreover, longstanding European empires and monarchies fell to violent mobs and revolutionaries—many of them spearheaded by men who would

---

4 Johnson, 9.

commit unspeakable atrocities against their own people. An Austrian lunatic came to control one of the most formidable armies ever assembled and used his political and military power to attempt to wipe out the Jews, brutalizing and killing six million of them before finally being stopped. Communist leaders such as Stalin and Mao killed tens of millions more. Finally, our new century opened with terrorists killing thousands of innocent civilians by flying planes into towers.

In our day, Revelation's patterns represented by the seals and their horsemen continue to play out. For instance, the COVID-19 pandemic is yet another iteration of the pestilence described by the fourth seal. Christ is exposing the emptiness of human power and beckoning us to give up worldly hopes. He has sent pandemics to cripple world powers before as a foreshadowing of his ultimate victory. In fact, the original readers of Revelation would have seen in Christ's breaking of the seals his ultimate authority even over the might of Rome. As one historian observed:

> Again and again, the forward march of Roman power and world organization was interrupted by the only force against which political genius and military valor were utterly helpless—epidemic diseases . . . and when it came, as though carried by storm clouds, all other things gave way, and men crouched in terror, abandoning all their quarrels, undertakings, and ambitions, until the tempest had blown over.[5]

Our world is anything but safe. We shouldn't be surprised by the tumult. But neither should we fear it. We can trust our Savior because we know he stands sovereign over all. The Lamb is breaking the seals and commissioning the horsemen to carry out his judgments. We know these trials ultimately come from the sovereign hand of our Lord, the one who will ultimately deliver his people.

3. Beware the Beast and the false prophet—governments who would devour the saints.

Human government is often an agent of good, an institution of common grace that orders society and keeps unrighteousness in check. Yet human government is also fallen, co-opted by the dragon to appease his bloodlust and wage war against the saints. In fact, the blessings of sound government are often the very thing Satan employs to promote the state as a false Messiah. As Johnson explains, "Rome had come to the rescue of some of the Asian cities [mentioned in Revelation 1–3] in time of need. It is no wonder that emperors, at least after death, were lauded in the eastern empire as 'lord and savior.'"[6]

State powers are often monuments to human hubris and achievement. Rome lauded itself as the ultimate power, demanding that its subjects affirm "Caesar is Lord." As "the Beast" in John's time, it promised stability, wealth, safety, and justice. Like every political institution and ideology, it promised utopia. But it also demanded devotion, even worship, from its subjects. It wanted to be seen as a savior.

As a result, Christians in the first century often found themselves at odds with Rome in particular and the culture in general—not because they were bad citizens but because they refused to engage in the civil religion of the empire. "Civil religion," notes Johnson, "seems so credible and satisfying, so affirming and nonconfrontational, so supportive of the social order and conducive to cultural harmony—as long as everyone docilely complies" (338).

This hubris and self-aggrandizing messianism ultimately characterizes every political entity. Utopianism is alive and well, a fact made clear every four years in our own political climate. Pastors and Christians must remember that the state beckons our worship. Like Rome, it too wants to be perceived as a savior.

What might Western, and particularly American, Christians learn from Revelation's depiction of the Beast and the false prophet?

First, while I deeply appreciate the innumerable social goods

---

5 Hans Sinsser, *Rats, Lice and History* (1934; reprint ed., New York: Bantam, 1960), 99. Quoted in Johnson, 124
6 Johnson, 337.

birthed out of America's political commitments, every Christian must recognize that the United States is not the kingdom of God, but part of the cadre of nations in Psalm 2 that rages against the Lord and his anointed.

Despite the evidences of common grace in the American political system (common graces worth preserving), we also see evidence of the Beast's image imprinted there as well. We find the Beast reflected in America's founding when it embraced a system of race-based slavery that considered black image-bearers only 3/5 of a person. We find that same bestial bloodlust today as the government upholds and funds institutions responsible for the slaughter of nearly 60 million unborn babies in the last 50 years, and as recently as *last year* failed to pass legislation protecting babies who survive abortion from infanticide.[7]

Second, Revelation teaches that the Beast's violence often manifests as state-sponsored persecution against Christians.

The Beast makes "war on the saints . . . to conquer them" (Rev. 13:7). While Christians in the West have yet to face this reality, we shouldn't assume it will never come, particularly given the pace of radical secularization. Our brothers and sisters in other parts of the world already experience this persecution. Western Christians would do well to note their faithfulness and willingness to suffer the Beast's violence for the sake of faithfulness to Christ.

More likely, Western Christians will find themselves objects of the false prophet's antagonism. State-sponsored false ideology—ideologies promoted with evangelistic zeal in university classrooms, television shows, hit songs, advertising, political campaigns, and the media—ultimately seeks either to deceive or displace Christians, removing them from any meaningful cultural participation. The false prophet "marks" the Beast's loyalists "on the right hand or the forehead"—symbolizing that they do his bidding (hands) and think in accord with his lies (head) (13:16). Those who won't follow suit and "get on the right side of history" are excluded from society, even kept from buying and selling—persecuted not by violence but through economic belittling (13:17).

It's easy to imagine how the LGBT revolution, now embraced and championed by Western governments, might lead to the very situation described in Revelation. We already see evidence along these lines as professors and public school teachers jobs' hang in the balance depending on whether they're willing to get in line with calling men women and women men.[8]

As Revelation teaches—and as history has shown—such social ostracization is Satan's endgame in state-sponsored deception.

Finally, Christians need to beware the Beast in how our nation's political movements and parties beckon our unswerving devotion, inviting us to view them as a savior. Political promises are often endowed with eschatological significance, the hope of heaven on earth. Political powers claim that they alone can fix the system, drain the swamp, or, at the very least, stop the other side from leading us to ruin.

Furthermore, the state uses military and technological power to posture itself as a messianic figure. Military might promises security while cultural achievements and technology promise comfort. As Poythress explains, a state's cultural achievements are turned from acts of servant leadership into invitations for spiritual devotion. "Technology," he writes, "becomes the worker of miraculous signs (13:14). The signs tell us that true power resides in the modern view of the world. Worship the power of the Beast, the power of the technocratic state organization, the power of the expert, because technology can work wonders like no one else."[9]

7 "Senate blocks bill on medical care for children born alive after attempted abortion," The Washington Post, Feb. 25, 2019. https://www.washingtonpost.com/politics/senate-blocks-bill-on-medical-care-for-children-born-alive-after-attempted-abortion/2019/02/25/e5d3d4d8-3924-11e9-a06c-3ec8ed509d15_story.html

8 "Professor Sues after University Requires He Use Student's Preferred Pronoun," National Review, November 5, 2018.https://www.nationalreview.com/news/professor-sues-after-university-requires-he-use-students-preferred-pronoun/; "'This Isn't Just About a Pronoun.' Teachers and Trans Students Are Clashing Over Whose Rights Come First," Time, November 15, 2019. https://time.com/5721482/transgender-students-pronouns-teacher-lawsuit

9 Poythress, 145.

Christians must resist the messianic claims of political figures and state power. I'm not asserting that Christians refrain from political action. By all means, give your political party your vote, just don't give them your heart. Again, as Johnson notes,

> The worship of rulers as gods, descendants of the gods, or gods in the making . . . is less overt in Western culture today than it was in the ancient world. Even in so-called secular states, however, governments can arrogate to themselves quasi-divine powers and issue quasi-divine promises of salvation to their loyal and believing subjects. Such states have no qualms about exploiting religious establishments in the interests of civic loyalty and cultural conformity. But people who, in allegiance to "another king, Jesus," resist the state's claim to ownership over forehead and hand, mind and deed, are seen as threats to good order and the common weal—and must be eliminated.[10]

Before moving on to the next point, let me quickly note that I don't mean to give the impression that state power is an unmitigated bad or that Christians should only have a negative posture toward government authorities. Obviously, both Genesis 9 and Romans 13 highlight that government is established by God, a common-grace institution that orders society and makes life possible in a fallen world. None of what John teaches in Revelation should be used against Paul's injunction that we both submit to the government (Rom. 13) and pray for its leaders (1 Tim. 2:1–2).

My burden in this article, however, is to show how John's apocalypse gives Christians a symbolic vocabulary that accounts for the deep-seated, Satanic evil which Christians encounter in political and cultural powers in every age, and how the vision of Christ reigning over history in heaven provides the church militant both marching orders for our age and an unconquerable hope in the age to come. Its stark good vs. evil dualism cuts through the fog of life under the sun, preserving Christians from Pollyannaish naivete.

American Christians have long known peace and prosperity. We would do well to let Revelation's symbolic world capture our imaginations for at least two reasons: first, our culture is growing increasingly hostile toward the church. Second, the pervasive dangers of materialism often go unnoticed in our hearts and churches. Revelation's portrait of the majesty of Christ emboldens Christians. The more we focus on Revelation's Christology, the more our churches will be marked by courage and fortitude in the winds of stiff opposition.

4. Beware the harlot of Babylon—forces that would seduce the saints.

The church's most insidious enemy is perhaps the harlot of Babylon, the promise of worldly pleasure at the expense of fidelity to Christ. Satan has devoured far more professing Christians' souls through sensuality and pleasure than social pressure and persecution. The harlot's seduction for material gain is often inextricably linked to the power of the state and its affluence (Rev. 17:3). Poythress summarizes the harlot's seduction well:

> The cities of the first century have not been the only centers of idolatry, greed, materialism, and sexual immorality. Our modern cities, with their wealth, false religions, and sexual exploitation, are modern forms of Babylon. The media and their advertisements can bring into our homes and thoughts the seductions of money, sex, power, and pleasure. Advertisements tell us that satisfaction and meaningful living can be found if only we buy the latest product. They say, "If only you have enough money and toys and sensual pleasures, you will be fulfilled."[11]

The church must resist the allure of personal affluence when that affluence demands we participate in unrighteousness. Worldliness, particularly

---

10 Johnson, 196–197

11 Poythress, 161.

the self-indulgent sort, is always a danger amid affluence. Of course, money and affluence aren't evil in and of themselves, but living for material wealth or embracing the spirit of materialism at the center of the secular worldview is.

According to John, seeking after the pleasures of the world is to leave the pure bride of Christ and wed yourself to the harlot of Babylon. But that harlot is destined for destruction. She may hold a cup made of alluring gold, but inside it are the "abominations and the impurities of her sexual immorality" (Rev. 17:4). Her beauty will be stripped, she will be publicly humiliated, and "in a single hour all [her] wealth" will be dry up (Rev. 18:17).

5. Remember who's coming.

Despite John's urgent and serious calls not to be taken in by political deceit or worldly pleasure, every chapter of Revelation rings with confidence that the church will prevail precisely because Christ has already conquered. No power threatens his regency. World history plays out by his command. Even the horsemen of conquest, war, scarcity, pestilence, and death are sent out by him to carry out his bidding (6:1–8). His victory over Satan is already secured (12:7–12), and one day he will come to dispatch the dragon's servants: the Beast, the false prophet, and the harlot. The Beast's power will prove vain, the false prophet's lies will be exposed (Rev. 19:17–21), and the harlot's hidden ugliness will come to light (Rev. 18:2).

None of this means churches should be characterized by triumphalism. Revelation reminds us that we are the church militant, at war against principalities and powers—awaiting our final rescue. Political turmoil should neither shock the church nor unsettle it but reinforce its identity as an embassy of a heavenly kingdom, one unwilling to capitulate to an old-world order that fawns at the pleasures of a harlot and worships the might of a Beast.

Resisting Satan's calculated snares and the allures of the world requires suffering. But throughout Revelation we're reminded that Christ turns Satan's attacks in on themselves. The Beast thinks he can slay Christ's people, but in reality his violence only causes them to "come to life" to "reign with Christ" (Rev. 20:4). Poythress again: "Even when demonic forces are ravaging the church, they are only establishing Christians in positions of real and permanent power!"[12]

Revelation reminds us that even in the midst of political and cultural upheaval, the church need not fear. It unfurls Satan's schemes and, in the process, gives Christians, particularly in times of increasing cultural and political opposition, a symbolic vocabulary to help them navigate their commitment to Christ.

Pastor, in this time of political turmoil, consider teaching your people Revelation. After all, our posture toward the world and its political institutions should be shaped by one great reality: *he is coming* (Rev. 22:20).

---

12 Poythress, 181.

ABOUT THE AUTHOR

Sam Emadi is a member of Third Avenue Baptist Church in Louisville, KY and serves as the Senior Editor at 9Marks.

Binding Consciences:

Brad
Littlejohn

There's no subject that got the Apostle Paul's dander up quite like Christian liberty.

The Epistle to the Galatians, which is largely dedicated to the topic, is full of exclamations like, "I am astonished that you are so quickly deserting him who called you in the grace of Christ and turning to a different gospel" (1:6) and "O foolish Galatians! Who has bewitched you?" This "bewitching" was the result of what Protestants have called "binding the conscience," which threatened to subject the Galatian believers to a yoke of slavery.

CHRISTIAN LIBERTY DISTINCT FROM LIBERTY

For modern Americans, there are few subjects that get *our* dander up quite like what we call "liberty." And for Christians, there's a grave danger of confusing the two—Christian liberty and political liberty. But there's in fact a very great distance between the two, a distance that the controversies over coronavirus have led many of us to lose sight of.

For some of us, we feel as through our liberty is being infringed upon anytime anyone tells us what to do. But for Paul, however, it was not *actions* that were the primary object of liberty, but *consciences.*

Consider the matter at stake in Galatians: circumcision. It wasn't the act of circumcision itself that Paul was concerned about, but what the Judaizers taught about *the meaning of the action*—that is was a rite necessary to salvation, an act that obedience to God demanded. For Paul, and for the Protestant Reformers, Christian liberty was threatened not by being told what to do—after all, authority may often need to tell us to do many things we'd rather not—but by being told *why* we needed to do it: *because God said so.*

ADDING OR SUBSTRACTING TO GOD'S COMMANDS

Of course, there are many things on which God *does* say so, many actions that God has commanded or forbidden in Scripture. Christian liberty, however, is threatened when any human being presumes to add to or subtract from God's commands—or, as Paul faced in Galatians, to continue to insist on commands of God that have now passed away in Christ.

Although the Roman Catholic Church explicitly claims the right to add spiritually binding commands beyond Scripture, Protestants tend toward subtler but no less dangerous violations of Christian liberty.

THE GAP BETWEEN PRINCIPLE AND APPLICATION

Quite often, we Protestants err not by manufacturing a wholly unbiblical demand out of nowhere, but by forgetting that there's often a wide gap between our principles and applications. Scripture warns us against gluttony, but it doesn't—in the New Testament at least—offer us a dietary code or a schedule for fasting. Scripture admonishes us to dress modestly, but it doesn't give us tips on when it's okay to wear skinny jeans. Scripture has something to say about the important differences between men and women, but not nearly as much as we might like it to.

Of course, I don't mean to say we should never answer such practical questions: any parent seeking to disciple their child cannot merely rattle off the fruit of the Spirit, but must seek to help their son or daughter think about practical ways in which God calls them to cultivate that fruit in their own lives. Anyone in authority must try to form conclusions about what love of neighbor requires in a situation and issue laws or admonitions accordingly.

But here's the problem: we're tempted to fill in these gray areas, to leap across this gap between principle and application, sometimes even pretending the gap doesn't exist. Rather than going through the hard work of moral reasoning and admitting just how many mistakes we might make in the process, we go straight from the principle to "The Bible says we must never do X" or "must always do Y" or "must do Z in this particular situation." We remove moral uncertainty and ambiguous authority from the equation by making it a simple matter of "you're either obeying Jesus, or you're not."

5 DANGERS OF WRONGLY BINDING CONSCIENCES

Whenever we do this, we risk *wrongly binding consciences*— naming something as clear sin that God's law has left us free to deliberate and disagree about. This can cause impressionable believers to stumble by making them equate a particular action with obedience to God, when in fact there may be multiple ways of faithfully obeying God on that issue.

Why is this dangerous— so dangerous that Paul angrily confronted the Apostle Peter over it? There are at least five dangerous responses that can result from such conscience-binding when it's not according to the Word:

1. Those of tender conscience may fall into needless fear that they're incurring God's wrath because they've failed to behave in a certain way.
2. Those who tend toward complacency may feel false assurance that they're spiritually alright because they, in fact, have toed the line of the outward behavior being condemned.
3. Those who are Pharisaical may be tempted to look askance at other Christians not following the command, and conclude, with smug satisfaction, that those "other believers" are less holy.
4. Those who are rebellious may feel an urge to disobey the command, however good advice it is, just because it has been framed as an absolute command.
5. Those who are wavering in their faith may see that the command is foolish or unreasonable, and since it is supposedly coming from Scripture, conclude that God must be a tyrant. Our culture today is full of men and women who left the church because they came to associate the faith with the arbitrary legalism or petty taboos of their church communities.

In all of these ways, attempts to bind the conscience outside of Scripture will tend to obscure the glorious gospel of justification and focus our attention on works of our own invention. And it's important to note that you can do this not merely by requiring what Scripture doesn't require, but also by forbidding what Scripture doesn't forbid. A pastor who tells his people that God *doesn't* want them wearing masks is violating Christian liberty; a pastor who admonishes compliance with government commands (which are directly only toward actions, and not consciences) need not be.

WHO CAN BIND A CONSCIENCE?

So we've seen what it means to bind the conscience and why it's dangerous. So who's at risk of doing this?

Some would say that only a pastor of a congregation, or someone in a position of formal authority over a certain group of people, can bind consciences, and even then only if they explicitly say, "The Lord commands this."

But this seems to me naïve. Let's start with the latter point. Human nature being what it is, it's easy for someone of tender conscience to hear something as a spiritually binding demand when it comes from someone in a position of spiritual authority. The pastor who preaches against tattoos might protest that he is simply *strongly advising* against them, not saying that each and every tattoo is a sin, but he must be mindful of how his words will be heard.

Likewise, in our age of mass media, we should realize that a great deal of authority—especially among evangelicals—is wielded at an informal level by Christian leaders who might pastor a church of only 500 but have an online audience of 50,000. The pastor who uses his position of great influence to make people think that obedience to Christ strictly demands some behavior that Scripture doesn't specify is in great danger of binding consciences—or at least unduly burdening them.

Indeed, one doesn't need to be an ordained pastor at all. Martin Luther spoke of the priesthood of all believers, and each of us is indeed called upon to preach Christ and his Word to one another. If we do so badly—perhaps by adding demands beyond Scripture—then we too are at risk of being like the Galatian Judaizers, especially if God has gifted us with significant influence or persuasive powers.

THE TEMPTATION OF SHORTCUTS

In any time of great conflict and confusion, we naturally look for clues on how we should act, whom we should listen to, and what God wants us to do. We're tempted in such situations to take shortcuts, to simplify the moral landscape before us, to grasp about for some relevant biblical principles, and to generate a formula for how all faithful Christians *must* respond.

We're right to want to know what faithful discipleship requires of us. We must defend Christian liberty without falling into relativistic complacency. But when we hastily conflate all our conclusions with all of God's commands, we endanger our own consciences and those of our brothers and sisters. "For freedom Christ has set us free; stand firm therefore, and do not submit again to a yoke of slavery" (Gal. 5:1).

ABOUT THE AUTHOR
Brad Littlejohn is the president of Davenant Trust.

Pastoring with Certainty in Uncertain Times

Zach
Schlegel

There are many truths we can know with certainty.

Luke gave his account of Christ's life to Theophilus "that you may have certainty concerning the things you have been taught" (Lk. 1:4). The apostle John wrote his letter "that you may know that you have eternal life" (1 Jn. 5:13; also, Rom. 8:38-39). Postmodernity might tell us truth is relative, but we know there are absolute truths we can be certain of—truths we must guard (1 Tim. 6:20) and be willing to suffer for (2 Tim. 1:12–14). Praise God for truth to stand on that's certain, reliable, and trustworthy.

Yet in our appreciation for truth and certainty, it's important to recognize God-given uncertainties.

The author of Ecclesiastes tell us that our pursuit of answers to many questions will end in "vanity" or "futility," like a vapor, breath, or puff of smoke (see esp. Eccl. 3:14). At the grand or meta level, God has kept some things secret (Deut. 29:29). At a more prosaic, everyday level, life confronts us with dilemmas that require nothing less than the wisdom of Solomon to resolve. Which mother would you have given the baby to (see 1 Kings 3)?

POLITICAL UNCERTAINTIES

Among the list of uncertain matters are so many of the political questions we face: Who's right on mask-wearing, reopening plans, or the vaccine? When will life be back to "normal"? What are the ongoing effects of slavery and Jim Crow? Whom do I vote for? Is there government overreach? Was that a political stunt or a legitimate issue? We live in a time with much uncertainty.

Yet the uncertainty surrounding such questions doesn't keep people from feeling certain about their convictions. Right now, the world is divided and dividing into smaller tribes. Each group lobs verbal grenades at each other. The divisions are accelerated by a 24-hour news cycle, social media, and being cooped up in quarantine. Rather than tread the waters of uncertainty, people look for something certain to stand on.

How do we pastor a congregation with conflicting sets of political certainties? How do we maintain the unity of the Spirit in the bond of peace" (Eph. 4:3) without compromising what's true?

TREADING WITH CAUTION

This is where we need to be careful. On the one hand, some will go beyond what God has made clear and certain. They'll claim certainty regarding a specific application of God's Word as the only way of faithfulness. They baptize their assessments of what's going on in the world. Really, they're saying they cannot be wrong. And members and leaders who do this will prove attractive to others. Again, who doesn't want certainty? The trouble is, they often prove to be quarrelsome, further entrenching sides in their positions.

On the other hand, we must not fail in our duty to preach the whole counsel of God and to help people understand what it means for their lives. To be sure, there are some political certainties. Discrimination is certainly wrong. Abortion is certainly wrong. And so forth.

Pastors and church leaders have to make decisions based on the information they have. But there's a difference between proud certainty and humble confidence. It's the knowledge that puffs up that leads to problems (1 Cor. 8:1). What if the thing we're looking for certainty in is something God has hidden? What if he intentionally left it as a disputable matter?

We should seek to understand what's going on in the world. We should scour the Scriptures for wisdom on every decision we make. In disputable matters, Paul instructs, "Each one should be fully convinced in his own mind" (Rom. 14:5b). But being "convinced in your own mind" does *not* give us permission to "despise" or "pass judgement" on those who disagree with us in those things (Rom. 14:3–4).

TWO KINDS OF WISDOM

We should also ask, which wisdom do you see in your own life and in those around you? There's a difference between "earthly" wisdom and "wisdom from above." Take a moment to read James 3:13–18 and consider the fruits of each type of wisdom.

Description of earthly, unspiritual, demonic wisdom (James 3:14–16)	Description of "wisdom from above" (James 3:13, 17–18)
· Bitter jealousy · Selfish ambition · Disorder · Vile practice	· Meekness · Pure · Peaceable · Gentle · Open to reason · Full of mercy · Impartial and sincere · Peaceful

James likely calls it "demonic" wisdom because it's an echo of Satan's lie in the Garden: that life is found in not in trusting God, but *being* God, "knowing good and evil" (Gen. 3:5). Ecclesiastes wisely reminds us of things we *can't* know—that there's such a thing as information God has withheld so that we might take refuge in him rather than grasping for the security blanket of trying to *be God*. Such humility produces an *openness to reason, a mercifulness*, and *impartiality* that helps us maintain the unity of the Spirit.

A FEW SHEPHERDING SUGGESTIONS

How can we shepherd the flock in times like these? Here are a few suggestions:

1. Preach and teach the Bible with certainty and conviction. You should have no fear in doing this. When people in turn share their "certain" convictions with you, you can always reply, "I'm not certain about that, but I am certain that Jesus is the way, the truth, and the life because the Bible tells me so."

2. Encourage people to assume the best in each other. In challenging times, we tend to assume the worst as a sort of defense-mechanism. Doing so doesn't promote unity; it hinders it. In 1 Corinthians 13:5, Paul says that love "keeps no record of wrongs." Strive to forgive, to keep no record of wrongs, and to assume the best.

3. Be the Lord's servant. This is what Paul calls us to in 2 Timothy 2:24–25. "The Lord's servant must not be quarrelsome but kind to everyone, able to teach, patiently enduring evil, correcting

his opponents with gentleness. God may perhaps grant them repentance leading to a knowledge of the truth." Include these things as a prayer list for your pastoral ministry.

4. Teach on the conscience and disputable matters. We need to know which hills to die on and which things we can disagree on and yet happily be members of the same church. Encourage folks to hold fast and refuse to compromise on gospel truths we can know with certainty; encourage them to be wary of teachers who claim certainty on issues that *are* disputable. Here are some books you can read or suggest on this topic:

- *Finding the Right Hills to Die On: The Case for Theological Triage*, by Gavin Ortlund
- *Conscience: What It Is, How to Train It, and Loving Those Who Differ*, by Andy Naselli and J.D. Crowley
- *Living Life Backward: How Ecclesiastes Teaches Us to Live in Light of the End*, by David Gibson

---

ABOUT THE AUTHOR

Zach Schlegel is the senior pastor of First Baptist Church Upper Marlboro in Upper Marlboro, Maryland.

Spurgeon's Preaching on Contemporary Issues

Geoff Chang   Alex DiPrima

One challenge preachers face is figuring out what to preach week after week. This was no different for Charles Haddon Spurgeon, the Prince of Preachers. Speaking to a group of pastors, Spurgeon once said, "All through the week I am on the look-out for material that I can use on the Sabbath." Spurgeon believed in the providence of God and saw a world full of important lessons for the observant Christian. He encouraged his students, "Always keep your eyes and ears open, and you will hear and see angels. The world is full of sermons—catch them on the wing." From time to time, this meant preaching sermons that were inspired by contemporary events of the day.

Spurgeon lived during a time of social and political upheaval. Throughout the British empire in the 19th century, there was no shortage of urgent news to lure a preacher's attention. However, Spurgeon didn't allow these matters to direct his preaching from week to week. In determining what to preach, Spurgeon was primarily driven by his own study of Scripture and his pastoral sense of his people's needs. His primary goal in preaching was to open up and apply the Scriptures to his people. As he reminded his students, "Those sermons which expound the exact words of the Holy Spirit are the most useful and the most agreeable to the major part of our congregations."

But on occasion, contemporary events so affected the life of his congregation that Spurgeon felt compelled to address these events. In these situations, Spurgeon still sought to preach God's Word, but he particularly sought to apply the Word to the issues of the day. Here in our day, pastors feel similar. We're confronted weekly with pressing news and events which vie for our attention. In response, pastors often wonder if and how they should address these issues from the pulpit. As we look at Spurgeon, what can we learn?

PREACHING AND POLITICS

Spurgeon generally avoided politics in his sermons. He didn't believe the pulpit was the place for political commentary or partisan wrangling. In 1873, after several years of publishing his sermons in the Metropolitan Tabernacle Pulpit, he wrote,

> Take the eighteen volumes of the Metropolitan Tabernacle Pulpit, and see if you can find eighteen pages of matter which even look towards politics; nay, more, see if there be one solitary sentence concerning politics, which did not, to the preacher's mind, appear to arise out of his text, or to flow from the natural run of his subject.

Spurgeon criticized the "minister absorbed in politics." In 1876, he said, "In proportion as the preaching becomes political, and the pastor sinks the spiritual in the temporal, strength is lost, and not gained." Thus, Spurgeon urged his Pastors' College students to avoid politics in their sermons. He wanted them to be known for gospel preaching, not political partisanship.

One reason Spurgeon was so opposed to political preaching was because he believed that the world wouldn't be changed principally through political policy or systemic reform, but through individual regeneration and widespread revival. He said to his congregation near the end of his life: "Great schemes of socialism have been tried and found wanting; let us look to regeneration by the Son of God, and we shall not look in vain." Clearly, Spurgeon's approach to social change was largely individualistic and focused on the necessity of the new birth.

We shouldn't overstate the case: Spurgeon was quite willing to speak to political issues that he believed intersected with biblical concerns. One notable example of this was Spurgeon's willingness to speak publicly against slavery in America, what he considered "the foulest blot" that ever stained a nation. Though slavery had been abolished for many decades in Britain, Spurgeon knew he had a large American audience and he did not hesitate to condemn the practice when appropriate,[13] even though it led to his sermons being burned in the American South. He also addressed the disestablishment of the state church, injustice for the poor and the oppressed, and certain matters related to British imperialism.

Whether in choosing to speak to political issues or in refraining, the preacher must not forget that he is to be a heavenly ambassador. In an 1873 article, Spurgeon wrote,

For a Christian minister to be an active partisan of Whigs or Tories, busy in canvassing, and eloquent at public meetings for rival factions, would be of ill repute. For the Christian to forget his heavenly citizenship, and occupy himself about the objects of place-hunters, would be degrading to his high calling: but there are points of inevitable contact between the higher and lower spheres, points where politics persist in coming into collision with our faith, and there we shall be traitors both to heaven and earth if we consult our comfort by sinking into the rear.

PREACHING DURING CALAMITIES

Spurgeon pastored his congregation through several significant crises on both a local and national level. In the spring of 1857, a violent revolt arose in the British province of India. By summer, shocking reports flooded back about horrific acts of brutality and murder that were committed on both sides of the conflict. A few years later, in December 1861, the whole Empire was stunned at the news of the sudden and unexpected death of Prince Albert, leaving Queen Victoria grief-stricken and desolate. Her reign would never be the same. Just a month later, a mining tragedy took place in Northumberland which resulted in the deaths of 204 men. In the first decade of his ministry, London was the epicenter of several cholera outbreaks, which also killed many. With the growth of foreign trade and market speculation, a financial panic struck on May 12, 1866. This decimated banks, industries, and the investments of countless of individuals. On these occasions and many others, Spurgeon's congregation and community were shaken by the reality of suffering, death, and loss. What did he believe to be his duty in such seasons? To proclaim the truth and hope of God's Word amid the calamities.[14]

---

13 For example, in preaching on "Presumptuous Sins" from Psalm 19:13, Spurgeon writes, "We, despite all that our American friends may say, are the freest people to speak and think in all the world. Though we have not the freedom of beating our slaves to death, or of shooting them if they choose to disobey—though we have not the freedom of hunting men, or the freedom of sucking another man's blood out of him to make us rich—though we have not the freedom of being worse than devils, which slave-catchers and many slave-holders most certainly are—we have liberty greater than that, liberty against the tyrant mob, as well as against the tyrant king."

14 For sermons on the above incidents, see "India's Ills and England's Sorrows" (https://www.spurgeon.org/resource-library/sermons/indias-ills-and-englands-sorrows/#flipbook/), "The Royal Deathbed" (https://www.spurgeon.org/resource-library/sermons/the-royal-death-bed/#flipbook/), "A Voice from the Hartley Colliery" (https://www.spurgeon.org/resource-library/sermons/a-voice-from-the-hartley-colliery/#flipbook/), "A Lesson from the Great Panic" (https://www.spurgeon.org/resource-library/sermons/a-lesson-from-the-great-panic/#flipbook/), and "The Voice of the Cholera" (https://www.spurgeon.org/resource-library/sermons/the-voice-of-the-cholera/#flipbook/)

So how did Spurgeon preach during these times? Though these sermons addressed the particular crises of the day, he didn't merely give a topical address on the disaster. Rather, he grounded his message in the Word of God. In picking a sermon text, he looked not only for relevant doctrines, but also for texts with a particular connection to the moment. For example, in response to the cholera breakout of 1866, Spurgeon preached on Amos 3:3–6 in which God warns Israel of the plagues he will bring on them, just as he brought upon the nations. During the revolt in India, amidst a time of national mourning, Spurgeon preached on Jeremiah 9:1 in which the prophet weeps over his people's suffering and sin. Spurgeon's belief in the sufficiency of Scripture meant that in each situation, God had a specific word for his people, and it was his job as a preacher to communicate that word.

Spurgeon was also careful to shape his sermon according to the text, rather than drifting off into personal commentary. In his sermon on Jeremiah 9:1, Spurgeon followed Jeremiah's example in weeping not only over the physical suffering of his people, but also over their moral ruin.

Similarly, on the day after the Great Panic of 1866, Spurgeon preached on Hebrews 12:27, "The removing of those things that are shaken, as of things that are made, that those things which are made, that those things which cannot be shaken may remain." Though everyone had the financial disaster in mind, his first three points dealt with the original context of the passage, namely the passing away of Jewish ceremonial signs for the permanent hope of the gospel. Only in the last two points did he move to the experience of loss. In every circumstance, Spurgeon believed that what people needed most in those times was to see themselves and their troubles in light of the truth of God's Word. These calamities, along with these sermons, provided an opportunity for them to do just that.

TWO COMMON THEMES

Though each situation presented its unique sorrows and challenges, two themes in particular arose in Spurgeon's preaching during calamities. First, Spurgeon emphasized the sovereignty of God. In a culture that was growing increasingly scientific and secular, suffering was explained away as simply the natural order of life. Even among Christians, the doctrine of God's sovereignty was falling out of fashion. But Spurgeon knew that it was one thing to speak about suffering theoretically. It was an entirely different thing to be in the midst of suffering. During times of suffering, abstract theories proved empty and people were longing for a stronger hope. Therefore, Spurgeon didn't hesitate to point people to the sovereignty of God—not only over blessings, but also over suffering.

Reflecting on the sudden death of Prince Albert, Spurgeon wrote,

> Whence came the fever? We could not suppose it to be bred, as the fever frequently is, in our courts and alleys in the plague-nest where filth provided it with all its food, until it was hatched to pestilence. What were its earliest symptoms, what its growth, and how it was that it baffled the physician's skill? We may lay aside these enquiries, to look apart and away from the second cause, to the first great cause who hath done all. "The Lord hath done it." He gave the breath, and he hath taken it away.

Far from being a source of fear, Spurgeon understood that the sovereignty of God brought hope for the Christian. He compared the naturalistic worldview to being raised by machines, rather than by a loving parent.

> It is as if a child should be left without nurse or parent, but then there is a cradle which works by machinery, and rocks the child so many hours a day; when it is time for the child to wake he is aroused by machinery; there is an engine ready to feed him. . . . When he comes up into life he is still fed by a machine; he sleeps, he goes on his journeys, in everything that he does he seen no living face, he feels no soft hand, he hears no loving tender voice; it is one

clever piece of soulless, lifeless mechanism that accomplishes all. Now, I bless God that is not the case with us.

God's people ought to believe that every calamity has come from God's wise and sovereign hand. So their response shouldn't be to complain or rebel, but to humble themselves and to renew their trust and dependence on God.

This leads to the second major theme of Spurgeon's preaching in calamity: clearly calling people to repentance. Reflecting on Jesus' words in Luke 13:1–5, Spurgeon believed that in every disaster, the appropriate response wasn't to try to find its root cause, but to repent, turning away from sin and turning to God in humble dependence. This isn't to say that we should ignore any practical lessons from the suffering. Spurgeon warned his people against foolish investments after the Great Panic. He reminded his people of the importance of proper hygiene during outbreaks. He spoke against oppressive governmental policies in the colonies. Ultimately, however, his preaching aimed at the individual's repentance before God. Earthly sufferings only pointed to the greater judgment of God to come. Therefore, all suffering doubled as a warning to repent.

Spurgeon rejected the teaching that specific instances of suffering could be traced to specific sins. Nonetheless, he believed that God brought suffering in order to awaken people to their sin, both individually and corporately. These calamities were God's holy judgment on the nation for their sins in a general sense, and they afforded the people an opportunity for reflection and repentance. For example, in his sermon during the Indian revolt, Spurgeon didn't focus primarily on the political issues of the British Empire. Instead, he preached against the drunkenness, licentiousness, and debauchery that characterized every level of English society. On other occasions, Spurgeon condemned the growth of ritualism in the Church of England, rationalism in nonconformist churches, and worldliness among churchgoers.

But in calling out sin, Spurgeon never left people in despair. He pointed them to the Savior. Preaching to a congregation that was wrestling with the frailty of life after the mining disaster, Spurgeon declared,

> Sinner, remember thy God shall live. Thou thinkest him nothing now; thou shalt see him then. Thy business now stops the way; the smoke of time dims thy vision; the rough blasts of death shall blow all this away, and thou shalt see clearly revealed to thyself the frowning visage of an angry God. A God in arms, sinner, a God in arms, and no scabbard for his sword; a God in arms, and no shelter for thy soul; a God in arms, and even rocks refusing to cover thee; a God in arms, and the hollow depths of earth denying thee a refuge! Fly, soul! while it is yet time: fly, the cleft in the rock is open now. "Believe in the Lord Jesus Christ, and thou shalt be saved." "He that believeth and is baptized shall be saved; he that believeth not shall be damned." Fly, sinner, to the open arms of Jesus! Fly! for he casteth out none that come to him.

CONCLUSION

Outside the pulpit, in his monthly magazine, *The Sword and the Trowel*, Spurgeon occasionally included articles that addressed contemporary political questions. Even then, his commentary on politics was generally limited to those issues that intersected with religious concerns. Nonetheless, it should be noted that Spurgeon generally believed his monthly magazine to be a more appropriate venue for political commentary. The preaching of the Word of God in the context of the gathered church required a narrower focus for Spurgeon. Preaching was for worship, edification, and evangelism, not for political analysis.

On the other hand, Spurgeon took advantage of widespread interest in current events to promote the preaching of the gospel. Occasionally, this meant taking advantage of holidays, popular trends, and other notable events and working them into his introduction or illustrations in order to connect with his hearers. These connections, however, would only be a small part of the sermon.

The challenge of preaching week-to-week continues for pastors today. What pastors choose not to preach on is just as important as what they choose to preach on. Like Spurgeon, pastors must exercise wisdom and discernment as they plan their preaching. The regular diet of the church should be the faithful exposition of the whole counsel of God. But on some occasions, pastors might consider deviating from their plans in order to give a more extended reflection on contemporary events. On all occasions, however, Christ must be proclaimed, for the salvation of sinners and the comfort of the saints.

ABOUT THE AUTHORS

Geoff Chang serves as an assistant professor of church history and historical theology and is also the curator of the Spurgeon Library at Midwestern Baptist Theological Seminary.

Alex DiPrima is the senior pastor of Emmanuel Church in Winston Salem, NC. He's a PhD candidate at Southeastern Baptist Theological Seminary and is currently writing on the social activism of C. H. Spurgeon.

A Primer on Conscience from William Perkins

Caleb Morell

"Wholesome laws of men, made of things indifferent, bind the conscience by virtue of the general commandment of God, which ordains the magistrate's authority, so as whosoever shall wittingly and willingly, with a disloyal mind, either break or omit such laws, is guilty of sin before God." William Perkins, *A Discourse of Conscience* (1596).[15]

"Human laws bind not simply, but so far forth as they are agreeable to God's Word, serve for the common good, stand with good order, and hinder not the liberty of conscience" William Perkins, *A Discourse of Conscience* (1596).[16]

I have often heard Mark Dever remark that the most profound Christian reflections on the conscience have come from the Puritans. Chief among the Puritans in this regard is William Perkins.

Perkins wrote voluminously, and his writings contain numerous treatises on the conscience.[17] Focusing almost exclusively on his earliest treatise, *A Discourse of Conscience* (1596),[18] this article aims to introduce contemporary Christians to the language of "conscience" by answering four questions and then applying them to the issue of civil disobedience and disputes among Christians. We will begin by asking,

1. What is the conscience?
2. What is Christian liberty?
3. What is "binding the conscience"?
4. What are "things indifferent"?

1. WHAT IS THE CONSCIENCE?

According to Perkins, the conscience is the faculty of the understanding which renders judgment by applying what one knows to be true to one's thoughts, actions, and affections.[19] He writes, "Conscience is a part of the understanding in all reasonable creatures, determining of their particular actions either with them or against them."[20]

As "God's arbitrator" within us, the conscience is constantly working to "give testimony or to give judgment."[21] The conscience renders judgment by determining "that a thing is well done or ill done."[22] As Perkins writes,

---

15 William Perkins, A Discourse of Conscience, in The Works of William Perkins, vol. 8. ed. J. Stephen Yuille (Grand Rapids: Reformation Heritage Books, 2020), 39. (Hereafter WWP)

16 WPP 8:40.

17 This presentation and discussion of Perkins' thought is based on William Perkins, A Discourse of Conscience Wherein is Set Down the Nature, Properties, and Differences thereof: as also the Way to Get and Keep a Good Conscience (Cambridge, 1596). See also Perkins' The Whole Treatise of The Cases of Conscience (1606). For further discussion see W. B. Patterson, William Perkins and the Making of a Protestant England (Oxford University Press, 2014), 90-113; and Coleman Cain Markham, William Perkins' Understanding of the Function of Conscience (PhD Diss. Vanderbilt University, 1967). Many thanks to Eric Beach, Brad Wilcox, Mark Dever, and Jonathan Leeman for their comments and help throughout.

18 WWP 8:39.

19 According to J.I. Packer, this definition of the conscience follows Thomas Aquinas' definition, see J.I. Packer, A Quest for Godliness (Wheaton IL: Crossway, 2010), 107). William Ames, for instance, begins his textbook on conscience by reproducing Aquinas' definition of conscience as 'a mans judgement of himself, according to the judgement of God of him' (William Ames, Conscience with the Power and Cases thereof (1643), 2. Cited in Packer, 107).

20 WWP 8:7.

21 WWP 8:10.

22 WWP 8:10.

"Herein conscience is like to a judge who holds an assize, and takes notice of indictments, and causes the most notorious malefactor that is to hold up his hand at the bar of his judgment."[23]

To render judgment, the conscience draws on the "mind and memory" to construct "practical syllogism[s]" with which to render judgment.[24] Such "syllogisms" go something like this:

> "Every murderer is cursed," says the mind.
> "You are a murderer," says conscience assisted by memory.
> Ergo, "You are accursed," says conscience, and so gives her sentence.[25]

Sometimes the conscience performs these reasonings before a sin, sometimes after.[26] In either case, the proper effect of such judgments is shame:

> The first [effect] is shame, which is an affection of the heart whereby a man is grieved and displeased with himself that he has done any evil, and this shame shows itself by the rising of the blood from the heart to the face.[27]

Shame is followed by "sadness and sorrow," then by "fear," then by "desperation," and finally, by the "disquietness of the whole man."[28] The point of all of this is to seek Christ, receive the gospel, and obey Christ's commandments.

This is where Christian liberty comes in.

2. WHAT IS CHRISTIAN LIBERTY?

Christian liberty, Perkins writes, is the "property of [a] regenerate conscience."[29] Through regeneration Christians are given a "good" conscience as opposed to the "evil" one they inherited through original sin.[30] This "good conscience" provides the Christian with assurance (or "certainty") of salvation. Perkins again: "[The] infallible certainty of pardon of sin and everlasting life is the property of every renewed conscience."[31] Through the gospel and the help of the Spirit of God, a regenerated conscience has a new syllogism with which to counteract the syllogisms of condemnation. Now the conscience testifies:

> "Everyone who believes, is the child of God."
> "But I do believe."
> "Therefore, I am the child of God."[32]

This is the promise of the gospel proclaimed in every Christian pulpit. And this is the work of every "good" conscience in every believer: first to *testify* that we are God's children (Rom. 8:16) and second to *excuse* or "clear" oneself against Satan's accusations. Perkins gives a hypothetical dialogue to describe the "good" conscience's work in responding to Satan's accusations:

> Devil: "You, O wretched man, are a most grievous sinner. Therefore, you are but a damned wretch."
> Conscience: "I know that Christ has made a satisfaction for my sins, and freed me from damnation."
> Devil: "Though Christ has freed you from death by His death, yet you are quite barred from heaven because you never did fulfill the law."
> Conscience: "I know that Christ is my righteousness and has fulfilled the law for me."
> Devil: "Christ's benefits belong not to you. You are but a hypocrite and want faith."
> Conscience: "I know that I believe."[33]

Christian liberty, then, is a summary of the Christian life. In Perkins' thought, it always goes hand-in-hand with "certainty of salvation."[34] As Perkins puts it, "Christian liberty is a spiritual and holy freedom, purchased by Christ" encompassing three things (and here Perkins tracks closely with John Calvin[35]):

---

23 WWP 8:12.
24 WWP 8:50.
25 WWP 8:50.
26 WWP 8:51.
27 WWP 8:52.
28 WWP 8:52-53.
29 WWP 8:57.
30 WWP 8:82. For "evil conscience" see Heb. 10:22. For "good conscience" see Acts 23:1, 1 Tim. 1:5, 19; 1 Peter 3:16, 21.
31 WWP 8:77.
32 WWP 8:77.
33 WWP 8:81.
34 WWP 8:57. As Perkins writes, "The second property of conscience is an infallible certainty of the pardon of sin and everlasting life" (8:61).
35 WWP 8:57. As Calvin writes in the Institutes,

1. Freedom from the *condemnation* of God's moral law.
2. Freedom from the *rigor* of God's moral law.
3. Freedom from the *bond* of the ceremonial law.

The first aspect of Christian liberty refers to the freedom from the guilt and condemnation of the law that comes through believing the gospel. "Christian liberty has three parts," Perkins writes,

> The first is a freedom from the justification of the moral law. For he who is a member of Christ is not bound in conscience to bring the perfect righteousness of the law in his own person for his justification before God. (Gal. 5:1–3).[36]

Through the gospel, every adopted child of God is "freed from the curse and condemnation of the law" (Rom. 8:1, Gal. 3:13).[37]

Secondly, every believer is freed from the *rigor* of God's moral law, "which exacts perfect obedience and condemns all imperfection."[38] Through union with Christ, God accepts our imperfect obedience, sanctifying it with Christ's perfection. "Hence it follows," Perkins writes, "that God will accept our imperfect obedience, if it is sincere."[39] God relates to us as his adopted *children,* not with an exacting demand for perfection but with the gracious affection of a father. Because of Christ, he accepts our obedience, however imperfect.

Thirdly, Christian freedom consists in freedom from the bond of the *ceremonial law,* which has been fulfilled by Christ. This frees the Christian to use that which was formerly forbidden under the ceremonial law (i.e. unclean meats) as unto the Lord. As Perkins writes, "Hence it follows, that all Christians may freely, without scruple of conscience, use all *things indifferent,* so be it the manner of using them is good."[40]

CHRISTIAN LIBERTY
Freedom from the condemnation of God's moral law.
Freedom from the rigor of God's moral law.
Freedom from the bond of the ceremonial law.

So we have seen how "Christian liberty" which is a gift of regeneration that provides freedom from condemnation comes through believing the gospel. But what does Perkins mean by "things indifferent"? What are they? How should they be used? And may they be forbidden or commanded?

3. WHAT ARE "THINGS INDIFFERENT"?

"Things indifferent"—or *adiaphora* as they are sometimes referred to—is a category for things not inherently right or wrong. "Indifferent" does not mean that they are of no consequence or that we should be apathetic toward them. Here the evolution of the English language has not been helpful. What the Oxford English Dictionary today renders "Having no particular interest or sympathy; unconcerned"[41] was as recently as 1828 defined as "Neutral, as to good or evil. Things in themselves indifferent, may be rendered evil by the prohibition of law."[42] The older definition is much closer to Perkins' meaning.

For this reason, we instead prefer to use the language of "morally disputable matters" when referring to what has historically been called "things indifferent." That these matters are "morally disputable" better conveys the nature of these discussions. As D. A. Carson has written,

> Today there is a tendency to refer to such *adiaphora* as "disputable matters" rather than as "indifferent matters"—that is, theologically disputable matters. On the whole, that terminology is probably better:

"Apart from a knowledge of [Christian freedom], consciences dare undertake almost nothing without doubting; they hesitate and recoil from many things; they constantly waver and are afraid. But freedom is especially an appendage of justification and is of no little avail in understanding its power" (Institutes, III.xix.1).

36 WWP 8:57.
37 WWP 8:57.
38 WWP 8:57.

39 WWP 8:57.
40 WWP 8:58. See Eph. 2:14–15, Col. 2:14.

41 OED Online. June 2020. Oxford University Press. http://www.oed.com/viewdictionaryentry/Entry/7179;jsessionid=61494FA30F6628009908C800D2210718 (accessed August 13, 2020).
42 Websters (1828).

in contemporary linguistic usage "disputable matters" is less likely to be misunderstood than "indifferent matters."[43]

For something to be "morally disputable" means that it is neither expressly forbidden or condoned by Scripture. As Perkins puts it, "things indifferent . . . namely such things as are neither expressly commanded nor forbidden by God."[44] Perkins specifically discusses fastings, eating meat, and recreation as examples of this category—hot topics among the Christians of his day as they sought to extract themselves from the rules of the Roman Church and return to Scripture.[45] Such matters are sometimes referred to as areas of "Christian liberty" because they frequently involve ceremonial laws that were in force in the Old Testament but no longer bind believers (i.e. food sacrificed to idols in 1 Corinthians 8, certain kinds of food in Romans 14, or Sabbath-observance in Col. 2:14). For such areas, Scripture gives principles, such as edification and love of neighbor, which guide the Christian to use them properly.

A proper understanding of "disputable matters" is central to Christian liberty because they must not be elevated to the status of God's moral law. As Perkins writes in *The Whole Treatise of Cases of Conscience* (1606), "It

is a part of Christian liberty to have freedom in conscience, as touching all things indifferent."[46] Again, this is not "libertine freedom" to do as one pleases, but freedom to use them as long as "the manner of using them is good."[47] As we will see, the category of "disputable matters" is especially important when we speak of binding the conscience.

4. WHAT DOES IT MEAN TO BIND THE CONSCIENCE?

According to Perkins, to bind the conscience is "to urge, cause, and constrain [the conscience] in every action, either to *accuse* for sin or *excuse* for well doing."[48] In a word, it is "to say this may be done or it may not be done."[49] That which "binds" then has "power and authority over conscience to order it," to command it.[50]

The question then, is who or what has authority to bind the conscience?

Perkins explains that the conscience may be bound "properly" or "improperly." The proper binder of conscience is the Word of God: "Proper is that

thing which has absolute and sovereign power in itself to bind the conscience. And that is the Word of God."[51]

Improper binding of conscience refers to *anything* or *anyone* other than the Word of God that asserts authority over the conscience. "The improper binder is that which has no power or virtue in itself to bind conscience."[52] As that authority belongs to God alone, any usurpation of that authority—whether by the Church of Rome or civil government—is unlawful.

Perkins could not be more clear on this point:

> But God is the only Lord of conscience because He once created it, and He alone governs it, and none but He knows it. Therefore, His Word and laws only bind conscience properly.[53]

> Therefore, the Word of God alone, by an absolute and sovereign power, binds conscience.[54]

"Disputable matters" cannot properly speaking "bind the conscience." As we have already explained, only God's moral law can properly bind the conscience.[55] We will delve further

---

43 D.A. Carson, "On Disputable Matters," *Themelios* 40.3 (2015): 383.
44 WWP 8:39.
45 WWP 8:33, 42, 58-59, 119, 327, 332, 343, 416.

46 WWP 8:395.
47 WWP 8:58.
48 WWP 8:13.
49 WWP 8:13.
50 WWP 8:13. "The binder is that thing whatsoever which has power and authority over conscience to order it. To bind is to urge, cause, and constrain it in every action, either to accuse for sin or excuse for well doing, or to say this may be done or it may not be done. Conscience is said to be bound as it is considered apart by itself from the binding power of God's commandment. For then it has liberty and is not bound either to accuse or excuse, but is apt to do either of them indifferently."

51 WWP 8:13.
52 WWP 8:26.
53 WWP 8:13.
54 WWP 8:13.
55 This is why the proper instruction of the mind and understanding in the Word of God was so important to Perkins. Without knowledge and understanding of God's Word, the conscience is bound to function improperly. An "evil" unregenerated conscience without God's Word is bound to make mistaken judgments. A "good"

into how consciences may be "bound" in "disputable matters" by the civil magistrate by virtue of the biblical command to submit to civil government (Rom. 13:1–2), but for now it is important to establish that only God's Word can bind the conscience.

THE ROLE OF MINISTERS IN BINDING THE CONSCIENCE

If only God's Word can bind the conscience, what role, if any, do ministers play in that process? In a word, through right preaching and proper instruction, God's Word binds consciences. Ministers are the means through which God works by his Word.

The first implication of this is to repudiate the Roman doctrine that the Papacy possessed the power to bind the conscience as a function of the power of the keys (Matt. 16:19).[56] "Here (say they) pointing to Jesus' words to Peter in Matthew 16:19, 'to bind is to make laws constraining conscience.'"[57] Perkins, however, disagrees. As we have already seen, binding the conscience is a sovereign power that belongs to God alone:

The sovereign power of binding and loosing is not belonging to any creature, but is proper to Christ who has the keys of heaven and hell. He opens and

no man shuts; He shuts and no man opens (Rev. 3:7).[58]

The role of the church and of ministers is to "publish and pronounce *that* Christ binds or looses," not to bind or loose by sheer *fiat*.[59] In this, Perkins interprets Matthew 16:19 in light of Matthew 18:15 where, according to Perkins, Jesus explains how "this binding stands not in the power of making laws, but in remitting and retaining of men's sins."[60] This authority, moreover, of declaring the good news of the forgiveness of sins is not restricted to the clergy but is given "to all Christians."[61] "God alone makes laws binding conscience properly, and no creature can do the like," not even ministers of the gospel.[62]

Ministers do not bind consciences. Ministers preach God's Word, which, when truly preached, binds the conscience.

ROLE OF THE CIVIL MAGISTRATE

The case of the civil magistrate presents an interesting opportunity to apply Perkins' categories. Christian consciences, Perkins explains, are bound by God's Word to obey civil magistrates by virtue of the sweeping command of God's moral law: "Whosoever resisteth the power resisteth the ordinance of God" and "they that resist shall receive to themselves judgment" and "ye must be subject not only for wrath, but also for conscience sake" (Rom. 13:2–5).[63]

Yet it is important to note that it is not the magistrate who binds the conscience by his law or decree but the Word of God which commands submission to magistrates. This distinction is subtle but important. The Christian does not need to conform the convictions of their conscience to the magistrate's decree; they just need to remember that they are commanded to obey the magistrate (Rom. 13) and submit.

Perkins insists that the magistrate does not possess "absolute authority" over our consciences, "for the sovereign power of God is incommunicable."[64] Instead, the magistrates power is a "finite and limited power" and only to be exercised in accordance with God's delegated authority.[65]

---

regenerated conscience poorly instructed in God's Word is likewise bound to make mistaken judgments. Only a "good" regenerated conscience that is properly instructed in God's Word will judge itself according to God's Word.

56 WPP 8:27.

57 Ibid.

58 WPP 8:27

59 WPP 8:27. Italics mine. " Again, this binding stands not in the power of making laws, but in remitting and retaining of men's sins, as the words going before declare, "If thy brother sin against thee" (v. 18). And Christ shows His own meaning when He says, "Whose sins ye remit they are remitted, and whose sins ye retain they are retained" (John 20:23), having before in the person of Peter promised them this honor, in this form of words, "I will give unto thee the keys of the kingdom of heaven, whatsoever thou shalt bind upon earth, shall be bound in heaven" (Matt. 16:19)."

60 WPP 8:27.

61 WPP 8:28: "Again, Origen, Augustine, and Theophylact, attribute the power of binding to all Christians, and therefore, they for their parts never dreamed that the power of binding should be an authority to make laws." One might detect a "nascent congregationalism" here. As Perkins has written elsewhere, the proper exercise of "binding and loosing," according to Matthew 18:15-18 and 1 Cor. 5:1-5 "must be done in the face of the church by the consent of the whole church" (WPP 4:246. Thanks to Eric Beach for pointing me to this reference).

62 WPP 8:35.

63 WPP 8:31.

64 WWP 8:35.

65 WWP 8:35.

Perkins' point is unmistakable: *no human,* no government, and no church can properly *bind consciences.* That is reserved for God's Word alone.

So what does this look like practically?

GETTING PRACTICAL

Laws Concerning "Disputable Matters"

In many cases, civil laws concern "morally disputable matters" such as speed limits and tax rates.[66] It is not that these are matters of no significance. It simply means that there is no positive command or prohibition in God's moral law concerning them. Such cases are simple: obey the law. Even though such civil laws have no power in themselves to bind the conscience, we are bound to obey them by virtue of the sweeping commandment of Romans 13: "Let every soul be subject to the higher powers" (Rom. 13:1). In other words, "They bind only by virtue of a higher commandment."[67] As a result, men are bound "in conscience to obey their governors' lawful commandments."[68]

But what about "Christian liberty"? Christian liberty means that we are freed from the condemning power of the law in order to fulfill the law by heartfelt obedience to God, who commands us to submit to the civil magistrate (Romans 13:1–2).[69] That leads to the first conclusion: if a civil law concerns "disputable matters," the Christian response is to obey.

Civil Laws and the Conscience	
Concern a "matter indifferent"	*Obey (Romans 13:1-2)*

Laws Affirming God's Moral Law

A second scenario could involve a civil law that confirms the moral teachings of Scripture. For example, a prohibition on murder (Ex. 20:13). If the civil law is rooted in part of God's revealed moral law (i.e. "thou shall not murder") then it is not the human law which binds but the divine law which is in force.[70] As Perkins writes,

> If the case falls out otherwise, as commonly it does, that human laws are not enacted of things indifferent, but of things that are good in themselves, that is, commanded by God, then they are not human properly but divine laws. Men's laws, entreating of things that are morally good . . . are the same with God's laws and, therefore, bind conscience, not because they were enacted by men, but because they were first made by God."[71]

Breaking such divine laws involves a "double condemnation" because it is breaking "that which is in conscience a law of God" and second, because in disobeying his lawful magistrate, he disobeys the general commandment of God touching magistracy."[72] That leads to the second conclusion, civil laws that affirm God's moral law are especially important to obey.

Civil Laws and the Conscience	
Concern a "matter indifferent"	*Obey (Romans 13:1-2)*
Affirm God's moral law as revealed in Scripture	*Especially important to obey*

When a Civil Law Contradicts God's Moral Law?

Sometimes, however, Christians face a situation where a civil magistrate establishes a law that contradicts God's

---

66 Perkins writes that this is the "ordinary sphere" of civil laws: "human laws properly entreat, namely such things as are neither expressly commanded nor forbidden by God" (WWP 8:39).

67 WWP 8:39.

68 WPP 8:39.

69 As the Dutch-speaking Strangers' Church in London put it in 1565: "Christian liberty is not a wandering and unruly licence, by which we may do or leave undone whatsoever we list at our pleasure; but it is a free gift bestowed upon us by Christ our Lord; by the which, the children of God, (that is, all the faithful,) being delivered from the curse of the law, or eternal death, and from the heavy yoke of the ceremonial law, and being endowed with the Holy Ghost, begin willingly of their own accord to serve God in holiness and righteousness" (Propositions or articles framed for the use of the Dutch Church in London, article 1. Reproduced in John Strype, The History of the Life and Acts of Edmund Grindal (New York, NY: Burt Franklin Reprints), 519).

70 WWP 8:39.

71 WWP 8:39.

72 WPP 8:39.

moral law, either by requiring what God forbids or by forbidding what God requires. As Perkins writes,

> When two commandments of the moral law are opposite in respect of us, so as we cannot do them both at the same time, the lesser commandment gives place to the greater and does not bind for that instant. Examples. (1) God commands one thing, and the magistrate commands the flat contrary. In this case which of these two commandments must be obeyed, honor God or honor the magistrate? The answer is that the latter must give place to the former, and the former alone must be obeyed. "Whether it be right in the sight of God to obey you rather than God, judge ye" (Acts 4:19).[73]

Perkins call for "civil obedience" is couched here in careful language. "Disputable matters" do not justify civil disobedience. Indeed, civil disobedience is only warranted if "we cannot do them both at the same time." In other words, all attempts must be made to *both* obey the Civil Magistrate and obey God.[74] Only when all options have been tried is civil disobedience warranted.

In such cases where the magistrate creates a law that contradicts God's law, the civil law does not bind the conscience, nor is the Christian bound to obey it. On the contrary, he is bound to obey God rather than man:

> But if it shall fall out that men's laws are made of things that are evil and forbidden by God, then is there no bond of conscience at all; but contrariwise, men are bound in conscience not to obey (Acts 4:19). And hereupon the three children are commended for not obeying Nebuchadnezzar when he gave a particular commandment unto them to fall down and worship the golden image (Dan. 3:28).[75]

And again,

> Moreover, in that man's law binds only by [the] power of God's law, hence it follows, that God's law alone has this privilege: that the breach of it should be a sin.[76]

In conclusion, only "the laws of God do or can do to bind conscience simply and absolutely."[77] Human laws, on the other hand, only bind "so far forth as they are agreeable to God's Word, serve for the common good, stand with good order, and hinder not the liberty of conscience."[78]

Civil Laws and the Conscience	
Concern a "matter indifferent"	*Obey (Romans 13:1-2)*
Affirm God's moral law as revealed in Scripture	*Especially important to obey*
Contradict God's moral law as revealed in Scripture	*Obey God rather than man*

A LINGERING PROBLEM

The unavoidable lingering problem from Perkins is that Christians often find themselves disagreeing about whether or not a specific moral question constitutes a "disputable matter" or an aspect of God's "moral law." It's easy enough to figure out what to do if you know what category you are dealing with. The first-century Christians had the advantage of knowing that the Mosaic food laws no longer applied (Rom. 14:14; Mark 7:19) and that debates over meat were therefore "disputable matters" to be dealt with according to the rules of 1 Corinthians 8 and Romans 14. We do not always have that same advantage.

We can "agree to disagree" about a matter of prudence when neither side takes the other to be in flagrant disobedience to God's Word. But if the parties can't agree as to whether or not the issue is one of biblical command

---

73 WWP 8:14-15.
74 WWP 8:14.
75 WWP 8:39-40.
76 WWP 8:40.
77 WWP 8:40.
78 WWP 8:40.

or a "matter indifferent," there doesn't seem to be any easy way of settling the dispute.

This poses clear challenges to church unity. Members who believe the issue to be one of God's moral law will often try to bind the consciences of those who think it to be a "disputable matter." These will in turn accuse the others of "legalism" and violating their Christian freedom.

How do we resolve these issues?

THE ROLE OF ELDERS

This is where a plurality of elders comes in. In the context of a local church, it is the elders' responsibility to interpret both Scripture and their church's Statement of Faith and Church Covenant to decide whether or not a specific behavior belongs in the realm of "disputable matters" to be endured or God's moral law to be enforced. In Perkins' day, these questions often involved whether ministers could wear vestments during religious services or eating meat on Fridays. In past generations and still to some extent today, they include dancing, music, and the consumption of alcoholic beverages. One particularly thorny issue among Evangelicals today is whether or not a Christian may permissibly vote for a Democratic candidate who, among other policy positions, is committed to defending and expanding abortion rights. Other examples might include in-vitro fertilization, attending a same-sex wedding, or watching an R-rated movie.

Some Christians will believe these to be morally binding aspects of God's moral law. Others will believe these to be "morally disputable matters" and call for "freedom" to disagree within the same church. If an issue belongs in the realm of "disputable matters" then it must be used with prudence for the glory of God, which means sometimes laying aside a "right" (Rom. 14:13, 1 Cor. 8:13). If it belongs in the category of God's revealed moral law, then ministers must teach their congregations how God's Word binds the conscience in that area. If a Christian persists in disobedience to God's moral law, they must be dealt with according to the rules of church discipline laid out in Scripture (Matt. 18:15–20; 1 Cor. 5:1–13).

WHO DECIDES?

The default position for most moral issues not explicitly addressed in Scripture is to treat them as "morally disputable." Nevertheless, the elders will frequently be required to examine an issue and render a biblical verdict on whether a specific moral issue belongs in the category of "morally disputable" or "God's moral law." Our elders at Capitol Hill Baptist Church have done so on issues such as divorce and remarriage, in-vitro fertilization, and attending a same-sex wedding.

This is part of the duty of being a shepherd: saying "no, that's not safe," or "proceed with caution," or "this is the right way to go."

If the leaders decide that a specific moral question belongs in the category of "morally disputable," then members of that church should submit to the elders' teaching and not attempt to improperly bind the consciences of other members by treating it as a matter of God's revealed moral law. If Joe feels that drinking alcohol is wrong, but the elders consider it "morally disputable," Joe should not go around telling other members of the church that Christians should not drink. At the same time, members who have "stronger consciences" should not abuse their freedom but walk in love according to the rules of Romans 14 and 1 Corinthians 8, which may mean sometimes abstaining from their "rights."

This also means that the elders of a particular church have the responsibility to discern whether or not a specific civil law involves a "disputable matter" and is therefore to be obeyed (Rom. 13:1–2) or a violation of God's "moral law" and civil disobedience therefore to be required (Acts 4:19). Again, these complex decisions will require careful examination of God's Word and the circumstances. Inevitably, some will disagree with the conclusions.

When the elders work hard to align their convictions with those of God's Word and clearly communicate to the congregation what issues belong in the realm of "things indifferent" and matters of God's revealed moral law, members will more readily know what issues they're deciding not to divide over, This allows them to more easily walk in love with one another. I hope this introduction to one Protestant Reformer on the topic of conscience will encourage Christians and pastors to work in their congregations to develop a shared language when discussing matters of conscience, Christian freedom, and civil disobedience.

ABOUT THE AUTHOR

Caleb Morell is a pastoral assistant at Capitol Hill Baptist Church and an MDiv student at the Southern Baptist Theological Seminary.

Publicly Praying for Government Authorities

Shane
Walker

You could hear a pin drop. The prayerful silence of our congregation grew even more still as I gave thanks for a politician and her role in maintaining the peace of the church. I then asked God that if she didn't know Christ, she would come to faith. I also asked that she would remember that on the last day she will give an account not to the Constitution and the law of the land but to the law of God.

After the service, several people approached me to tell me in a hushed voice that the politician was certainly not saved. She was, it turns out, a very public sinner. My understanding is that at least one visiting family never returned because they believe I sinned grievously by even suggesting the possibility of her salvation.

Praying publicly for politicians can be hard. I remember one Sunday I thanked God for the new mayor. Upon saying "amen," I looked up only to discover that her former opponent had just taken a seat in a nearby pew.

All public prayers have three audiences: God; ourselves (Ps. 42:11); and our listeners, saved and unsaved (Ps. 22:23), including political leaders (Ps. 2:10, Ps. 82).

Even so, almost every Sunday in the pastoral prayer, I pray for a variety of political figures at all levels and branches of government. Because such prayers are fraught with the possibility for offense—and because I feel my own temptations to play the prophet or be unduly political—I often wonder: why bother praying publicly for politicians? There are so many reasons *not* to do it. But they're insufficient. Why? Simply put, because God commands it.

> But seek the welfare of the city where I have sent you into exile, and pray to the LORD on its behalf, for in its welfare you will find your welfare (Jer. 29:7).

> First of all, then, I urge that supplications, prayers, intercessions, and thanksgivings be made for all people, for kings and all who are in high positions, that we may lead a peaceful and quiet life, godly and dignified in every way (1 Tim. 2:1–2).

Both the New Testament (1 Pet. 2:11) and the Old Testament (1 Chron. 29:15, cf. Heb. 11:16) teach that believers are sojourners on earth, exiles from the heavenly Jerusalem. We are to pray "for the welfare of the city" in which we find ourselves. Our temporal welfare—and to a degree our spiritual comfort— are dependent on the political and economic order in which we live.

THE PEACE OF THE CHURCH

Paul not only commanded Timothy to pray for political leaders, he also told him why: "that we may lead a peaceful and quiet life." We're commanded to pray for the peaceful conditions that allow the church to gather publicly and individual Christians to live openly as followers of Jesus. These conditions create what I refer to as the "peace of the church."

This peace can show up in a variety of historical and political circumstances. It's easy to see in settings where governments recognizes religious freedom, but we should also pray for it—especially pray for it—where governments don't and would otherwise arrest Christians on account of their faith. To pray for this peace does not commit believers to political systems, parties, or candidates. It requires simply that we pray.

Further, we are to make "supplications, prayers, intercessions, and thanksgivings . . . for all people, for kings and all who are in high positions." In supplications, intercessions, and thanksgivings we find the importance of shared welfare. We want to pray so that if the politician (or that politician's opponent) were listening, he or she would recognize how it benefits everyone (Eccl. 10:20). Part of the way we recognize our common welfare is by identifying how God is using authorities for our good.

Thus, Paul can complement King Agrippa on his familiarity "with all the customs and controversies of the Jews" (Acts 26:3). We can also assume that Paul found reason to give thanks even for Nero. The emperor's resumé included matricide, incest, gay marriage to the surgically transitioned "female" Sporus, megalomania, devaluation of currency, and claims to deity. He was also a failed pop and sports entertainer. Nero either personally or through proxy was responsible for Paul's martyrdom. And yet Paul charged Timothy to give thanks even for Nero.

Believers should never thank God for wickedness. Rather, we should thank him for his good purposes in sovereignly governing such sin. Paul could have thanked God for Nero's beautification of the city of Rome, his introduction of fire safety standards for buildings in the capital, the continuation of the peace of Rome, the blessings of Roman citizenship (see Acts 25:25), and the internationalization of the Empire allowing for the spread of the gospel through the world (see Col. 1:6). Both Peter (1 Pet. 2:13–14) and Paul command us to find reason to give thanks for all political leaders.

POLITICAL PRUDENCE IN PRAYER

In the Old Covenant, God's people were created to function within a system of government regulated by God's word and within specific geographic boundaries. The nation of Israel could not fully obey the law outside of the Promised Land (Ps. 105:44–45). New Testament church polity, however, is designed to function under all forms of government. The church can gather and worship at almost all levels of religious freedom.

Crafting a pastoral prayer for political leaders, then, must take into account current political conditions. The peace of the church enjoyed in the United States allows me to pray for the salvation and conversion of politicians, and reform in the judiciary and law enforcement. It allows me to petition for national revival, and for Christians to vote according to biblical principles. I can give thanks for pro-life politicians, for those who support Judeo-Christian morality, and for politicians with testimonies of being born again.

These freedoms are taken for granted. They're not open to all Christians. In places where the peace of the church is more fragile or even non-existent, the pastor must approach public prayer for those in authority with greater care. We don't know the exact petitions that Ezra and his contemporaries used to obey King Darius' command to pray for "the life of the king and his sons" (Ezra 6:10). But we can assume that the content of their prayers didn't appear threatening or politically destabilizing to the king or his informants.

That's not to say that public prayer should not be animated by servile fear before the state, nor grant any ground to a government who would declare itself sovereign over Christ or slow the spread or clarity of the gospel, as some nationals parties would have it.

Still, "this is the will of God, that by doing good you should put to silence the ignorance of foolish people" (1 Pet. 2:15). Believers should publicly do good so as to overthrow false and negative stereotypes.

PRACTICAL CONSIDERATIONS

If your church has never prayed for politicians, then perhaps teach your people the practice before starting. In the churches I've served, a brief word on 1 Timothy 2 prior to your first prayer would be enough. At the very least, include this verse in your prayer: "Lord, you tell us in your Word to intercede for kings and all who are in high positions, that we may lead peaceful and quiet lives. And so we pray for Mayor Jones…"

In the United States we have a federal system comprised of municipalities, county/parish, state, and federal levels. I personally view voters as authorities and pray for them corporately before elections. Each level of government has both elected and unelected officials, and in general I pray for elected officers by name and the other authorities by office. This allows me to pray for teachers, law enforcement, the military and their chaplains, civil servants, and the judiciary. You may find it a helpful exercise to list all elected officials voted on by the members of your congregation and pray for them on successive Sundays.

Praying for authorities can accomplish a lot of good in your church. First and foremost, it demonstrates obedience to God.

It sensitizes us to how God uses such men and women for his good and wise purposes.

It allows pastors to exhibit care for the shared welfare of the church and state officials.

It provides pastors the opportunity to remind congregations of their civic responsibilities.

It models for others how to pray about complicated topics, which is useful for both family worship and other public prayer meetings.

Lastly, it offers you a winsome bridge to the gospel should you ever meet with those whom you've prayed for. You can tell them of the many times your congregation has given thanks for them and interceded before the throne of God on their behalf. As Paul reminds us, the Lord "desires all people to be saved and to come to the knowledge of the truth (1 Tim. 2:4), and that would have been true of even Nero.

ABOUT THE AUTHOR

Shane Walker is the preaching pastor of First Baptist Church in Watertown, Wisconsin.

How to Hold Your Tongue About Politics And Thereby Not Split Your Church Over Things the Bible Doesn't Talk About

Greg Gilbert

Okay, so maybe there's a little more to say about this topic than just a cheeky emoji. Especially in this *annus horribilis* which is 2020, the entire world and everything in it seems to be swallowed up in the gaping maw of political fighting. I was talking with a friend the other day, and we both lamented that neither of us could remember the last time we had a conversation that wasn't about pandemics, protests, or people pining to be president—all of which, of course, is patently political. To make matters worse, the pressure on pastors to publicly give their opinion on every event that explodes into the Twitterverse is enormous. To some, silence is violence, and a failure to speak tells us everything we need to know. To make matters even *worse*, let's be honest—most of us, even as pastors, *do* in fact have opinions about most of these things, sometimes strong ones. And given that it's our *job*, week in and week out, to speak, to teach, to persuade, it sometimes feels entirely natural and right and good—even *necessary*—for us to wade into every controversial conversation with the goal of setting folks straight.

All that said, I'm actually not here to say that pastors should never speak about "the political." Sometimes our very charge to communicate the teachings of the Bible will *require* us to speak about issues that larger society has decided to appropriate into the political conversation. After all, abortion is a political issue. The definition of marriage is a political issue. Justice is a political issue. And those are all things, at one level or another, that the Bible also speaks to. Because of that, it wouldn't be "prudent" to say, "Well, I don't talk about political things." It would in fact be a dereliction of duty to deliberately avoid them; to do that would be to refuse to speak what the King has spoken.

So here's the question I want to address here: "What are some guardrails that can help a pastor navigate 'political issues,' especially in a year like this?" I can think of four that I've found helpful.

1. STAY OFF SOCIAL MEDIA. JUST STAY OFF.

Twitter, Facebook, Instagram, All of Them—are cesspools of bad-faith, angry, unedifying screaming when it comes to political exchanges. The fact is, you will *never* convince someone of the rightness of your political opinion in a thread of 280-character tweets, nor even in a Facebook post. So just stay off of it; don't get in social media arguments; stay out of the fray. Think of it like this: If you're a pastor, then the Lord has given you a platform and an authority that the vast majority of people on Facebook simply do not have. So use that platform! When you speak to these issues, let it be from your pulpit, with the full authority and (hopefully) carefulness that commands.

If staying off social media pretty much entirely isn't an option for you, let me at least offer one more piece of advice. This is a point I've made not only to pastors, but also to my own congregation: Part of the problem with social media is that we all think our tweets are on the edge of going viral, and therefore we all think our opinions are a hair's breadth away from moving the needle on the national political scene. But if we're honest with ourselves, we'll realize pretty quickly that very few of us have that kind of influence; our tweets and posts *aren't* going to move the national needle. But you know what they *could* do? They could cause a detonation in the community closest to us; they *could* blow up your church. So whether you're a pastor or a member of a church, consider above all what your tweet or post might do *in and to the life of your church*. Those are the people most likely to read it, to be offended by it, to shoot back at you for it—or to start sniping at each other over what you said. And consider: Is your tweet more likely to do measurable good for your political cause, or to do measurable bad in the life of your church? And isn't the unity and peace of the church more important than your eyeball-scratching need to share your 🔥🔥 opinion on the latest Twitterfight *du jour*? Almost always, the answer to that question will be a resounding YES.

2. PREACH THE BIBLE, NOT THE HEADLINES.

In other words, remember your charge as a pastor and preacher of God's Word. Your authority to speak extends to—and *only* to—that which is spoken by God in his Word, the Bible. To be sure, the Bible speaks about a lot of things; in fact, it speaks to the most important questions of human existence, and those are always the kinds of questions that tend to get politically hottest. We'll talk about that more in a bit. The point I want to make here, though, is that it's critical for you to remember where your authority lies. It lies in the Bible, and therefore you should make every effort to limit your public pronouncements to what the Bible says and to straightforward applications of those truths.

Just by the way, all this is but one more argument for preaching expositional sermons through entire books of the Bible. Instead of your sermon topics being driven by whatever is in the headlines, you'll simply preach what's next in the text. Sometimes you'll find that that "next text" is *crazy* relevant to the headlines. Other times, you'll find that the Lord wants to direct your church's attention elsewhere. But the point is that the Word sets the agenda, not the world.

Here's my point: if you commit to being a pastor who remembers his charge, who steps into the pulpit each week and says what the Bible says, you'll be something unique and powerful—a herald of the King of heaven. But if you involve yourself in every fight, using the pulpit to address every question that explodes into the headlines, you'll become something else entirely—just one more braying, politically-opinionated donkey in our current national shoutfest. So I charge you in the presence of God and of Christ Jesus, who is to judge the living and the dead, and by his appearing and his kingdom: Preach the Word.

3. DISCERN THE DIFFERENCE BETWEEN BIBLICAL PRINCIPLES AND POLITICAL POLICIES.

Now, obviously, preaching and applying the Bible like that requires wisdom. One kind of unwise pastor will be so fearful that he won't even say what the Bible says because he's afraid it will be heard as "getting into politics." Another unwise pastor will extrapolate from the Bible to whatever he really wants to say—you know, how the laws of warfare in Deuteronomy actually mean that it's ungodly to prohibit citizens from owning nukes, or how the Year of Jubilee actually means God wants all property to snap back to government ownership every 49 years, or whatever. As a wise pastor, though, you should try to avoid that kind of tenuous extrapolation: Say what the Bible says, and then apply it straightforwardly in first-order applications. That's the way of pastoral wisdom.

Ultimately, this kind of wisdom consists in being able to

discern the difference between biblical principles and political policies. So it's one thing to say, "Every human being is made in the image of God," but it's quite another to say, "and therefore this proposal by Congressman Whoever should become law." The fact is, the Bible lays down a ton of clear, non-negotiable principles for which it's *not clear at all* what specific *policy* would be the exact best way to pursue to uphold those principles.

So, for example, the Bible speaks clearly to the truth that unborn babies are made in God's image. But what's the best *specific policy prescription* to save unborn lives? Is it appointing justices to the Supreme Court, or changing laws, or creating certain economic incentives and safety nets? Or is it all that? Similarly, the Bible speaks clearly to the truths that God created and values ethnic and cultural diversity. It speaks clearly to the fact that he hates oppression. But what's the best *specific policy prescription* to address racial tensions in America? Is it justice system reform, or the payment of reparations, or something else entirely?

A wise pastor will realize that his authority *certainly* extends to insisting on the principles laid down by God's Word, but *seldom* to insisting on any one particular policy prescription.

4. HOLD THE CENTER.

A few weeks ago, a nationally known Christian writer published an article lamenting the fact that few if any of our national political leaders seem to have any interest in "holding the center." What he meant by that was *not* just holding a compromise position on every issue, trying to get the porridge just right. What he meant, rather, was that most everyone in the country right now, even its political leaders, seem to be fleeing to the extremes of political ideology and rhetoric, and mostly just flinging slogans at one another and forcing every development in the news into the service of their political aims. So what the nation lacks right now—and what it desperately needs, this author said—are leaders who, instead of fleeing to the edges, will seek to "hold the center"—that is, who will say what is true regardless of whether it helps or hurts a particular political cause.

That author is exactly right, and part of the charge God gives to pastors is to "hold the center" in just that way. Again, that doesn't mean always being silent, it doesn't entail a hard-core "spirituality of the church" position, and it doesn't mean simply picking the middle-of-the-road, milquetoast compromise position on every question. What it means is fighting the temptation to the run to the extremes, and learning to speak truth according to the Word wherever you see it and in every direction. Say what's true on this side of the conversation, say what's true on that side, and say what's true that *neither* side is saying.

Further, learn to say those truths without slogans. In fact, avoid political slogans at all costs, and say what's true in your own words. Ultimately, the goal ought to be to speak in such a way that *every Christian* has to say, "Yeah, that's hard to disagree with, and he has every right to say it because it's biblical truth."

Part of your charge as a pastor is to avoid the temptation to run to one extreme and lob rhetorical grenades at the other side. Rather, commit to standing in the center of the chaos—planting your feet on the Word of God—and speak truth wherever you see it.

CONCLUSION

This is a hard year to be a pastor. There's the pandemic. There's the frustration, for many of us, of not being able to gather with the church as normal. There's the vaguely ridiculous prospect of preaching to a congregation whose faces you can't see because they're all wearing masks. There's the livestream you launched literally two weeks after you publicly called down God's own curses on yourself if you *ever* consented to a "video venue." There's the civil unrest boiling in many of our nation's cities. There's the fraying patience of our church members, and our own deep sense of decision-fatigue. There's the demand by frankly everyone to "Do something!" and "Say something!" And irritating and aggravating all of this like an Old Testament hairshirt, there's the presidential election. This is a hard year to be a pastor, and frankly, it doesn't much look like it's going to get easier anytime soon.

So what's a pastor to do? Here's the best I've got: Remember the office you hold. Remember where your authority lies. Remember your charge. The fact is, you're not a politician, you're not a pundit, you're not a get-out-the-vote lackey for a political party, you're not a social media "influencer," whatever that is. You're a herald of the King of Heaven, and as such, you hold a special authority and charge to speak for him. So say what he says, no more and no less, and remind your people that this world is *not* all there is—no matter how much this world may want to make them forget that.

ABOUT THE AUTHOR

Greg Gilbert is the Senior Pastor of Third Avenue Baptist Church in Louisville, Kentucky.

Should Pastors Endorse a Candidate?

Bobby Scott

If you live in the United States like me, you know we live in divided times—not just in our nation, but also, sadly, in the church. Christians publicly spar in the public square, perhaps particularly over the upcoming presidential election. A seemingly unbreachable chasm stands between the "Never Trumpers" camp and the "You aren't really saved unless you vote for Trump" camp.

This impasse raises a question, Who *can you* vote for? And *that* question leads to another question: Should a pastor step into the melee by endorsing a presidential candidate?[79]

Before you endorse a candidate, here are several questions you should consider. And though I'm primarily addressing pastors in the United States, the principles below apply anywhere.

IS IT WITHIN A PASTOR'S JOB DESCRIPTION TO ENDORSE A POLITICAL CANDIDATE?

Well, kinda yes and kinda no. Pastors have a broad range of responsibilities. But they don't need to be well-versed in American politics in order to faithfully fulfill their calling. Christ charges pastors to shepherd a local church.

More specifically, a pastor should preach the Word so that he equips the saints for the work of the ministry. He must lead the church to stay on mission to save sinners from the world's fallen kingdoms (Acts 2:38–40; 1 Tim. 4:16), which is a different calling than leading the church to save fallen kingdoms. By equipping the saints, the pastor prepares church members to be salt and light in their communities. He equips believers to labor for what's just and right in their different vocations, as unto Christ (Matt. 6:10). This is yet another way Christians, as servants of our King, show compassion for the lost and love our neighbors until Jesus returns and makes all things right.

Pastors must disciple their congregation to care about the common good (Jer. 29:4–7). In our representative democracy, Christians can bless their neighbors by voting for what's good and for leaders who will promote flourishing. Every community has different needs, and how its citizens vote will reflect those different needs. Pastors, therefore, need to know and be able to teach their respective congregations Jesus' Kingdom politics.

In principle, this includes helping your people understand *what kind* of leader to vote for and *what kind* of issues to prioritize. Pastors who do this well are undergirded by the driving conviction that *every* government is God's servant (Rom 13:1-7)—that no matter who wins an election, King Jesus is still on the throne (Prov 21:1; Dan 4:34–36). Pastors must resist the temptation to politicize their pulpits with partisan

---

79 For another helpful resource on this topic, consider checking out Jonathan Leeman's Politics and the Pulpit (Part 2): Pastors and Political Candidates (erlc.com)

politics as if the outcome of a presidential election will be a death-blow to the church and her mission. No oligarchy, dictatorship, monarchy, aristocracy, republic, compromised democratic government, or bad president can stop Jesus from building his church (Matt. 16:18; John 6:37, 39).

HOW DOES BEING A CITIZEN OF JESUS' KINGDOM INFLUENCE A PASTOR'S DECISION TO ENDORSE OR NOT TO ENDORSE A POLITICAL CANDIDATE?

Jesus said, "My kingdom is not of this world. If my kingdom were of this world, my servants would fight" (John 18:36). Paul agreed, "For our citizenship is in heaven, from which we also eagerly wait for the Savior, the Lord Jesus Christ" (Phil. 3:20). The Father transfers all Christians into Christ's Kingdom (Col. 1:13).

Christians aren't American citizens first and foremost, or the citizens of any nation. We're Kingdom citizens first, and our primary mandates come from King Jesus (Acts 17:7). In our American representative government, disciples directly influence our nation by electing leaders who, Lord willing, promote good, punish evil, and lead with integrity. Our Christ-given identity requires this of us. We therefore should use our voting privilege in ways that allow the church to peacefully pursue our King's mission of making disciples (Matt. 28:16–20; Acts 1:8; 1 Tim. 2:1–2).

Our mission is urgent and of the utmost priority. God has stamped an expiration date on our national work visas. Christ's Kingdom has already broken in, so too has the countdown to his return and the consummation of his kingdom. However important an election may be, pastors must be careful not to overstate their case. The moment they do, people will be distracted from hearing his gospel. Simply put, pastors aren't called to rescue earthly kingdoms by mobilizing the saints to be king-makers. We *already have* a good King, and so pastors proclaim to the nations that this good King's name is Jesus (Ps. 2:12; John 18:37). He grants dominion on earth to whomever he wishes (Dan. 4:32), and he humbles and removes whatever rulers he wishes (Dan. 5:25–28).

God may use everything from local elections to global pandemics to raise nations high or bring them low. He is the Sovereign, and he leads all nations as he wills. The United States is no exception, and pastors urging their congregants to vote for either *culturally religious conservatives* or *culturally compassionate progressives* won't save our nation. We don't need nation-wide reform; we need nation-wide repentance brought about by prophetic preaching (Jer. 18:7-11). If this is true—and the Scriptures say that it is!—then it's immeasurably more important for pastors to preach the Word and call for our nation and its leaders to repent (Jonah 3) than it is for them to convince their congregations that their candidate will save America. The same is true for pastors everywhere.

American pastors who extol America's greatness but never mention her sins and her need to repent are more like Israel's failed prophets (Jer. 23:21–22) than the faithful shepherds God calls them to be (Jer. 23:4). Pastors, don't see this upcoming presidential election—or any election in the future—as an opportunity to take America either back to its alleged "good ol' days" or forward to a progressive utopian future. Instead, keep your church riveted on the King's mission: equipping the saints to preach the gospel of the kingdom, calling our nation to repentance, and praying that God may perhaps bring a national revival in which he will use us to save people from every ethnic, cultural, and national background (Rev. 5:9).

WHAT IS THE COST OF ENDORSING A POLITICAL CANDIDATE, AND IS IT WORTH IT?

To win the battle for African-American Civil Rights, Rev. Martin Luther King, Jr. placed his liberation political theology at the forefront of the black church and the nation. Through his efforts, America made great social progress—progress that was an unqualified blessing.

But the legacy of King's politicizing the church with the social gospel has been far from good. For example, at the recent funeral of Civil Rights leader Rep. John Lewis, Rev. Raphael Warnock, the current senior pastor of King's former church, Atlanta's historic Ebenezer Baptist Church, asserted, "We celebrate John Lewis. He *was* wounded for America's transgressions, bruised for our iniquities; the chastisement for our peace *was* upon him, and by his stripes we are healed. So let's remember him today." That's blasphemy. Genuine disciples have Jesus and his penal substitutionary atoning work at the center of their worldview. We cross a bright red line and pay far too steep a price when we make the pulpit the centerpiece for proclaiming partisan politics rather than for proclaiming Jesus as King of the nations. No matter how tempting, the church cannot promote partisan politics to bring about social change at the cost of biblical fidelity.

But allowing political means to justify the end isn't only a problem in the black church. The rise of the Religious Right and the Moral Majority of the 1980s married a good portion of the evangelical church to Republican politicians in order to combat America's decaying culture. James Dobson became one of the most feared men in national politics. A simple appeal from his radio program would flood phone lines in Congress, pressuring officials to vote according to Christian values or else face a backlash in the election booths. On some level, this seems to directly contradict Paul's admonition that Christians not fight with carnal weapons (2 Cor 10:3–4).

Even today, conservative evangelical leaders ally with cultural conservatives who are trying to save America. Sadly, this practice often impairs the witness of the church (1 Thess. 4:12a). Pastors pay a price for tethering their good Christian witness to both the good and bad of a presidential candidate.

For example, Sidney Blumenthal, a critic of Republicans, wrote:

> Reagan opposed the Civil Rights Act of 1964, opposed the Voting Rights Act of 1965 (calling it "humiliating to the South"), and ran for governor of California in 1966, promising to wipe the Fair Housing Act off the books. "If an individual wants to discriminate against Negroes or others in selling or renting his house," he said, "he has a right to do so."[80]

Reagan's racist attitude was caught on a hot mic in 1971 when he joked to President Nixon, calling African UN delegates "monkeys." When white evangelical pastors hail Reagan as our greatest president ever,

---

80 "Reagan's Race Record," The Atlantic, cited by Matthew Yglesias. November 9, 2007.

they often put a stumbling block in front of their black brothers and sisters in Christ.

In our two-party democracy, pastors who endorse a specific candidate must count the cost of such endorsement. A pastor can carelessly divide Christ's church over public presidential endorsements. By endorsing a candidate, a pastor attempts to do all the thinking and discerning for his people. God's people don't need that. Instead, they need pastors to disciple them to think Christianly, pastors who trust that their members will carry out those Christian commitments when they vote.

Of course, there may be times when a pastor must exhort the church to vote for or against a specific presidential candidate. For the sake of argument (and putting aside eschatological debates), what pastor *wouldn't* tell his congregation to vote against the Antichrist? Conversely, if another Daniel appears, and he was running against three criminally corrupt administrators (Dan. 6), then wouldn't it be wise for a pastor to encourage his congregation to vote for him?

There's also a third option— one that I pray pastors and Christians will more soberly consider. When our two-party voting system only presents two options of varying degrees of evil, at some point we need to say "enough is enough" and recognize that the lesser of the two evils is still too evil.

As our nation grows darker, Christians need to make sure that we aren't compromising our light by voting for what's dark. Some might say we're already there. Some might not. Right now, that approach may not be what's best for America. But in the end, it may be far more beneficial for our witness before the world.

For any pastor troubled by how members of his church may vote in November, instead of using your pulpit to publicly endorse a candidate, perhaps it would be better to patiently disciple your congregation toward Christ-like maturity. Pastors, whatever you do this election season, let's strive to unite the church around Jesus by preaching that He is our King.

He had no predecessor
and He'll have no successor
There was nobody before Him
and there'll be nobody after Him
You can't impeach Him
and He's not going to resign
That's my King!
Do you know Him?
(Because knowing Him
changes everything)
— S. M. Lockridge

ABOUT THE AUTHOR

Bobby Scott is a co-pastor of Community of Faith Bible Church in South Gate, California.

Hey Pastor, Has Anyone Ever Told You You're a Good Listener?

Dan Miller

Some aspects of our current political turmoil are relatively novel. The level of intensity is not among them. In the mid-nineteenth century, for instance, political conflicts precipitating civil war polarized churches. In the mid-twentieth century, churches found themselves in the middle of civil rights battles, anti-authoritarian foments, the sexual revolution, and the legalization of abortion. The political tensions of our day may seem strident in comparison with the preceding 40 years, but they are nothing new under the sun.

What's unprecedented now is the degree to which political tensions divide members of the same local church. Today's docket of political tensions—racial justice, police reform, intersectionality, even coronavirus—divide godly people seated in the same pew. Layered onto these topics, the anti-abortion candidate in the next election sports an extensive list of egregious moral failures, spawning contentious debate among the saints concerning his qualification for office.

As pastors strive to maintain peace in the midst of such political turmoil, let's remember that navigating division is nothing new. Indwelling sin ensures that every assembly of saints, to one degree or another, constitutes an arena of relational turmoil—politically or otherwise. Loving relationships are hard-won and demand the church's capacity to navigate strong differences of opinion. Members of a healthy local church must learn to employ an array of strategies to pursue love and unity across our divides—divides which pale in comparison with those Jesus' death has already bridged (Gal 3:28; Eph 2:11–22; 3:6).

Chiefly, church members must commit to listening to one another. Love leans forward and listens. Prideful, selfish ambition towers over and trumpets. For the sake of God's glory and the unity of our local churches, learn to be a listening pastor. As we do, here are four things to remember.

1. WE LISTEN TO A GOD WHO TALKS AND TALK TO A GOD WHO LISTENS.

We are made in the image of a God who speaks and hears. God spoke the world into existence and uses the medium of human language to reveal himself to his people. Idols, by contrast, are deaf and dumb. "They have mouths, but do not speak . . . ears, but do not hear" (Ps 115:5–6). Those who worship false gods become like them (v. 8). Those who worship the living God speak to him and heed his Word.

What does this mean for listening to others? A life spent heeding God's Word—"making your ear attentive to [God's] wisdom" (Prov 2:2)—habituates the soul to listen to others. Listening to God requires the humility of looking outside myself for life-giving truth and the discipline of applying God's truth in my daily life, even when that proves painful. Walking with God naturally orients me toward humble, attentive listening to those made in his image.

Pastors who struggle to listen well betray some level of failure when it comes to listening well to God. How often have we witnessed such spiritual declension when yet another disgraced pastor stops listening to others? Whether fueled by pride, greed, sensuality, or laziness, an early sign that a soon-to-fall pastor has stopped listening to God is that he stops listening to the wisdom of the saints God has placed around him. He dismisses the wisdom of fellow elders or church members who attempt to hold him accountable, push back against his self-serving ideas, or rightly question his motives. These ear-plugging habits are rooted in an ear-plugged relationship with God. They'll eventually bear the bitter fruit of prideful, inattentive dismissal of what others have to say—particularly when what they have to say is what God has been saying to him all along. Listening to others is a spiritual muscle we exercise in the gymnasium of private devotion to God.

2. WE LISTEN TO ONE ANOTHER TO KNOW ONE ANOTHER.

Listening is more than a strategy for information transfer. To listen to someone is to learn about someone. For the believer, listening to God's Word is life itself (Deut. 32:45–47). God's Word reveals his heart to me, thereby drawing me to love him with all of mine (Deut. 6:4–5). From the other direction, as God listens to us, the goal is more than our psychological comfort. By inviting our prayers and petitions, God invites us to join him in redeeming our broken world in light of his future promises—to resist the world that is, in the assurance of what will be (Matt 6:10; Acts 4:23–31). In other words, by hearing God's Word and praying to him we come to know him.

In a similar vein, we come to know others, in part, by listening to them. Even if we hold divergent opinions, even if we lend our ear to an unfair critic or a muddleheaded opinion-monger, listening permits us to peer into the window of their soul. Love welcomes such opportunities. We may find the window smeared with self-deceptive, dishonest, or banal speech. But listening allows us to know someone more fully. Therefore, love rejoices to listen.

Pastors must repeatedly remind themselves of this. After all, it's easy to listen to the member of the flock who believes as you do or shares your interests. It's easy to hear words of respect and appreciation from kindred spirits. But our Lord loved us while we were his enemies, and your Christian brother or sister, no matter how difficult they are to endure, is no enemy. They are saints chosen by Christ and united to his body by his shed blood. Love listens in order to know them.

Listening also helps me know myself. Whenever a believer is willing to discuss contentious, divisive issues with me, I must receive it as a gift. Even if what they say is painful to hear, even if the conversation seems to produce no lasting good, it is ultimately a gift. Most criticism contains at least a grain of truth we need to hear. May God help us learn to blow away the clouds of emotive resistance by listening attentively in order to see ourselves more accurately, and thus realize the sanctifying effect God intends for us .

3. LISTENING WELL TO OTHERS INVOLVES FOCUSED CONTROL.

Some witty bloke observed that God created us with two ears and one mouth, so we should listen twice as much as we speak. Perhaps this folksy proverb found inspiration in James' exhortation to "be quick to hear and slow to speak" (Jas. 1:19). I suspect we pastors are typically more wired to preach on that text than obey it. But being quick to hear is not a self-help suggestion from a postmodern life-coach. It's a command from the Holy Spirit.

As a lot, pastors typically register on the verbal end of the communication scale. We like to talk so much that we do it for a living. Sociological studies claim that public speaking is one of the most prominent human fears—yet, weirdly, we welcome what most people find terrifying. As a result, we often hear about pastors' preaching skills. But how often have you heard that a pastor is a superb listener?

Brother pastors, we prioritize speaking over listening at a scandalous rate. We're commissioned to talk and we must. But we shouldn't permit this calling to excuse poor listening. May God help us grow in the discipline of holding our tongues and opening our ears.

4. LISTENING WELL TO OTHERS IS NOT THERAPY.

When God listens, he's always up to something. By contrast, our world promotes an almost wholly passive listening in which listeners are mere "sounding boards" to help speakers discover their own wisdom.

Biblical listening isn't like that. It doesn't imply that we put on an earnest expression and an affirmative smile while grunting agreement no matter what is said. That type of listening treats the speaker as sovereign and fails to recognize that we must simultaneously listen to God whose word is supreme in every conversation.

Jesus listened well. He epitomized the Spirit's command: "Be quick to hear and slow to speak." But having listened, Jesus usually had something to say. Sometimes encouragement, sometimes rebuke, sometimes a word of guidance, sometimes prayer. We're not Jesus, of course, but we should emulate him by listening with a love that is willing to respond for God's honor, whether we must rebuke (Matt. 16:21–23), warn (Luke 22:31–34), say nothing (Matt. 27:11–14), redirect (John 21:20–22), or save the day (John 21:15–17).

Love leans in and listens well. May God help us so love one another.

ABOUT THE AUTHOR

Dan Miller is the senior pastor of Eden Baptist Church in Burnsville, Minnesota

Pastoring Amid Suspicion

Tony
Shepherd

Some years ago I lived in Nashville, and like many creatives in Music City, I worked at a studio. One morning a sound engineer accidently keyed in the wrong code to the alarm system, triggering a very loud and embarrassing siren. I was able to shut the system down, and I assumed the police would soon be on their way to investigate. No problem, I'll just explain what happened and things will be fine.

A few hours went by with no police showing up, so I figured they recognized it as a false alarm. By the end of the day I had forgotten all about the mishap. As the sun set, I began to shut down the studio and head to my men's Bible study. I cut the lights and started shoving studio equipment into my backpack. That's when I heard it—the sound of voices in the front lobby. Suddenly, a flashlight pointed in my face. Two police officers were there, following up on a call that an alarm went off.

"Officers", I said, "that alarm triggered hours ago." It looked bad. There I was in a dark room shoveling expensive gear into my backpack. Should I tell them that I was on my way to a men's fellowship? Would that arouse more suspicion? Maybe I can give them a number to call to verify that I'm the lawful operator of the building? By God's grace, I got out of that situation without anyone getting hurt. My story checked out and they let me go. But it didn't feel good to be in the hot seat of suspicion, even for a moment.

As pastors, we face many situations where people are suspicious of us. Sometimes the world suspects that pastors are in it for the money and the influence. That may be true for some, but not most. Besides, we can usually shake off the suspicion that comes from outside the church. But what do we do when suspicion spreads *inside* the church?

As a country, we're facing difficult times. The political climate is extremely polarizing, particularly with a presidential election around the corner and the social temperature dialed up on account of issues surrounding racial justice. All this, of course, is happening while the COVID-19 pandemic rages on, prompting controversies over states' rights, personal freedoms, left-wing and right-wing agendas, and vaccines. All these issues have fostered an environment where suspicions grow and nuance goes out the window. People are either "far-left liberal Marxists" or "far-right racists." The prospect of charitable dialogue seems to get farther out of reach.

Of all people in the world, our churches need to be places where these issues can be discussed in a God-glorifying way. Even more, our churches need to be places where people learn to practice the one anothers even through disagreements on polarizing topics.

So how do we pastor our churches toward health and unity in this current environment of suspicion?

THE ROOTS OF OUR SUSPICION

There's a difference between discernment and suspicion. Christians should always discern truth from error and right from wrong based on the objective standard of God's Word (Heb. 4:12). Discernment waits for the facts and judges accordingly. But suspicion is often "intuitive" and subjective. It judges based on assumptions, perception, or hunches. It often impugns motives.

The reason we tend to be suspicious toward one another is because we have hearts that are prone to suspicion toward God. In the beginning, God gave us everything we needed. We were made in his image. We had fellowship with him and fellowship with one another. God even put us in a perfect world where everything was good. God blessed humanity and gave them permission to enjoy the bounty of his created world. The only exception was that we were not to eat of the tree of the knowledge of good and evil. That was the only "no" in a sea of "yes!"

The story takes a radical dive when the serpent takes God's one "no" and made it seem as if God were stingy. "Did God actually say, 'You shall not eat of any tree in the garden'? . . . For God knows that when you eat of it your eyes will be opened, and you will be like God, knowing good and evil" (Genesis 3:1, 5). The serpent wanted humanity to entertain the notion that God is not entirely trustworthy. Maybe he's hiding some good thing from us. Maybe he's lying. But that lie had deadly consequences. In the Garden and ever since, the human heart still tends toward suspicion of both God and others.

HOW TO FIGHT A CULTURE OF SUSPICION

Let's consider a few points on how to fight a culture of suspicion in our local churches.

First, repent of suspiciousness toward God.

"This is the message we have heard from him and proclaim to you, that God is light, and in him is no darkness at all" (1 John 1:5). God is not in the business of deception. God is light. His heart is pure, and all of his ways are true. On top of that, he gave us his Son as the propitiation for our sins. We have no reason to be suspicious of him.

Second, suspect your own heart.

"If we say we have fellowship with him while we walk in darkness, we lie and do not practice the truth" (1 John 1:6). Not only should we uphold God's character as true, we should also humbly embrace the reality that it is *our* hearts that are prone to wander. *We* are prone to hypocrisy and every kind of self-deception. There's a healthy kind of Christian self-examination and self-suspicion that clears the way for the next step (see also Matthew 7:3-5).

Third, confess your own sins.

"But if we walk in the light, as he is in the light, we have fellowship with one another, and the blood of Jesus his Son cleanses us from all sin" (1 John 1:7). True Christian fellowship emerges as we search our own hearts and confess our failings one to another. Hostility abounds in a culture where everyone is busy calling out each other's shortcomings to the exclusion of their own. Yes, there's a time to confront others' sin. But the time to confess our own sins is *always.* As we come to each other with a posture of humility and confession, we build the kind of relational integrity that enables us to have healthy dialogue about weighty and often polarizing topics.

Finally, lovingly give one another the benefit of the doubt.

"Love is patient and kind; love does not envy or boast; it is not arrogant or rude. It does not insist on its own way; it is not irritable or resentful; it does not rejoice at wrongdoing, but rejoices with the truth. Love bears all things, believes all things, hopes all things, endures all things (1 Cor. 13:4–7)." Love has a posture of grace. Loving one another well doesn't mean rejoicing in a lie. It doesn't mean we shun discernment. Love rejoices with the truth. Complex conversations about politics, race, and justice need the truth of God's Word. Love also gives one another the benefit of the doubt. It "believes all things" by holding out the possibility that those we disagree with have a measure of God's grace working in their lives that I may not have working in mine. Love comes with an eagerness to sustain our life together at any cost short of embracing lies or evil. This kind of love sustains a healthy congregation.

The current cultural moment is tumultuous, and having honest conversation about polarizing topics is a difficult task for any church. But we can fight suspicion as we repent of our own suspicions of God, confront the darkness of our own hearts, confess our sins to one another, and pursue love. May the Lord give us grace to foster a culture like that in our churches for his glory alone.

ABOUT THE AUTHOR

Tony Shepherd is the Associate Pastor of Hampton Roads Fellowship in Newport News, Virginia, and former Christian Hip-Hop producer for Lecrae, Shai Linne, Trip Lee and others. Tony is husband to Jolene, and father to three wonderful sons and a beautiful daughter.

Live with Your Church Members in an Understanding Way

Michael Lawrence

In the first years of marriage, my wife and I had a recurring conversation. We'd each come home after a long day's work. She'd ask me how my day was, and I'd say "Great." Being a thoughtful young husband, I'd ask her how her day was, and she'd launch into a detailed narrative. I would happily listen and when the narrative paused, offer my suggestions and solutions to the problems she'd described. Sometimes her response was appreciative, often it was slightly irritated, but usually she was frustrated to the point of tears because I "wasn't listening."

It took a while, but I finally learned that she wasn't sharing her day with me so that I could solve her problems or offer advice. She was more than capable of dealing with the office politics and technicalities of her job. She was rehearsing the day with me so that I could understand what she'd experienced and be with her in the feelings those experiences had provoked. Having been apart all day, she was inviting me back into her life. In quickly offering solutions and advice, I was effectively ignoring her and focusing on her job. No wonder she was frustrated with me!

Surely this is part of what Peter meant in his instructions to husbands:

> *Husbands, in the same way, live with your wives in an understanding way, as with a weaker partner, showing them honor as coheirs of the grace of life, so that your prayers will not be hindered.* (1 Pet.3:7)

One of the ways husbands love their wives is by sympathetically understanding thcm, entering into their experience as women and wives and honoring them by according that experience the dignity and weight it deserves. Your wife's life is not a problem to be solved but an experience to be shared.

That insight had a profound impact on my marriage. But this isn't an article about marriage. The principle Peter employs has a wider application. Who among us doesn't want to be understood? Who doesn't feel loved when someone simply takes the time to listen and appreciate our joys or sorrows? And there are so many contexts where we put this principle to work, often intuitively:

- We don't explain to the grieving that their loved one's death was all part of God's eternal plan. We sit with them in their grief and save the theology lesson for later.
- We don't lecture the family whose house burned down on the importance of smoke detectors. We take them in for the night and shelter them in their shock.
- We don't lecture the teenager who missed the varsity cut that she should have practiced harder. We share

her sorrow and remind her how much we love her and believe in her.

- We don't congratulate the bride and groom with reflections on how hard marriage is. We celebrate and rejoice with them.
- We don't berate our child for being afraid to jump in the pool even with their "floaties" on. We stand below them with outstretched arms, assuring them we'll catch them.
- We don't respond to a black friend's fear over police shootings with statistics about the larger number of white people shot every year. We listen, ask questions, try to understand, and bear the burden with them.

Does that last example seem as obvious as the others? That's what this article is about.

Is God sovereign over death? Are smoke detectors important? Does practice pay off? Is marriage hard? Do flotation devices work? Are more white people shot by police than black people? Yes. But is that really the point in any of those situations? No. The point is how the person feels in that moment, and what it means to love them by understanding those feelings and meeting them there. Sometimes that means listening, sometimes encouraging or reassuring, sometimes participating with them, but almost never does it mean explaining

how the feelings are wrong. At that moment, the feeling is the most important fact you need to know if your goal is love. And your goal should be love.

Why is a principle that's so obvious and intuitive in most of life so difficult to apply when it comes to our political life? Why is it so hard to see and love the person in our local church who's fear, or grief, or anger seems to be contradicted by our political persuasions? Why would we think that grief over a loved one's death or a child's fear of the pool should be met with tender compassion while a brother's grief over racism or a sister's fear of police brutality should be answered with political arguments or statistical explanations? Why are the facts of those feelings so easily dismissed? Could it be that politics and policy controls our identity in those moments more than the gospel? Could it be that our politics has reduced the brother or sister to a problem to be solved rather than a person to be loved?

Because the local church is the body of Christ, Paul reminded the Corinthian church that "if one member suffers, all the members suffer with it; if one member is honored, all the members rejoice with it" (1 Cor. 12:26). In a similar context, he reminded the Roman church, "Love one another deeply as brothers and sisters…Rejoice with those who rejoice; weep with those who weep. Live in harmony with one another" (Rom. 12:10,16). No doubt

the churches in Corinth and Rome were as diverse ethnically, socially, and politically as any of our churches today. No doubt they disagreed with each other over how to understand and respond to the pressing political and social issues of their day. No doubt the privileges and oppressions of the Roman empire fell unequally on their various members. But Paul reminds them, and continues to remind us, that our compassion, love, and understanding toward one another isn't based on our common political persuasions or social experience but on our communion with each other in Jesus Christ.

Living with our fellow church members in an understanding way as we move toward a divisive election this November doesn't mean giving up our political persuasions or abandoning our policy proposals. Loving one another doesn't mean that we never talk about current events. Understanding one another doesn't mean that we're not allowed to disagree. Sympathizing with someone's feelings doesn't mean endorsing their political views. It certainly does not mean giving someone permission to re-interpret Scripture or place themselves beyond the critique of Scripture because of their experience. Scripture interprets our experience and feelings, not the other way around. It does mean paying loving attention to the person whose politics you disagree with but whose communion you share. It means treating their feelings with tenderness and respect because those feelings are usually the first and most important facts you will encounter, and their feelings are not up for debate. Instead, those feelings are an invitation and opportunity to understand and enter into the experience of a fellow member of the body of Christ and to bear their burden with them whether or not you agree with the cause of that burden or its solution.

It took a while for me to learn the lesson of living with my wife in an understanding way. Thirty years later I'm still learning to listen first, understand deeply, and only then offer my counsel or perspective. But along the way I've learned that listening earns a hearing because it demonstrates my commitment to her rather than to myself and my solutions. It also changes the counsel and perspective I offer, because it's been affected by what I've heard.

Should it be any different in the church?

Pastors, wading into the conflict surrounding elections, social unrest, immigration policy, and police reform might seem like something to be avoided at all costs. You might feel ill-equipped, out of your lane, and perhaps encumbered by your own political convictions. But if you're anything like me, you spend a lot of time speaking into marriages, teaching husbands how to love their wives and wives how to honor their husbands. You've spent years honing the skill of helping men and women listen to each other, understand each other, and love each other despite their differences and disagreements in the context of the family. Take heart. You have everything you need to do the same for the spiritual family you've been called to shepherd. Teach them to live with one another in an understanding way. Listening well and loving deeply won't resolve every political disagreement in your church. It will do something better. It will reveal that your people are Christians, because of the way they love one another (John 13:35).

ABOUT THE AUTHOR

Michael Lawrence is the senior pastor of Hinson Baptist Church in Portland, Oregon.

How Love Paves the Way for Hard Conversations

Garret Kell

We recently had a difficult family meeting. Our kids had been acting disrespectfully, so we sat down in the living room to talk it out. Hard words were shared; tears were shed. Though it was not a comfortable confrontation, the kids knew we shared our hard words in love. How? Because that same living room is normally where we play games, wrestle, read Scripture, sing songs, dance, and tell stories. That room is known *mostly* for enjoyable love. So when we sit down to have unenjoyable conversations, they may not like it, but they never doubt our love for them.

A healthy church should be like a living room. What normally marks its relationships is thoughtful encouragement (Heb. 3:13), Scriptural instruction (Rom. 15:14), hopeful songs (Eph. 5:19), glad thanksgiving (1 Thess. 5:18), weeping together in grief (Rom. 12:15), joyful testimonies (Ps. 66:16), generous hospitality (1 Pt. 4:9), and welcoming fellowship (Rom. 15:7). When churches are rich with this sort of love, it strengthens relational equity that supports hard conversations.

In recent months, our church has needed this kind of strength. We've had lots of particularly difficult conversations. By difficult, I mean we've needed to say hard truths to people we love.

"We have serious hesitations about your relationship with that person."

"It appears your ambition for money and affirmation are driving you into dangerous territory."

"Your social media presence is not honoring to Jesus and is provoking division."

"You're treating your spouse in ways you wouldn't treat an enemy."

"We fear your thinking is being more informed by the news and social media than Scripture."

"Your apathy toward others' suffering is gravely concerning."

"We're compelled to warn you that your sinful pattern is leading you toward judgment."

In isolation, these statements could sound harsh, judgmental, and condemning. But in the context of loving relationships, God can use these words to give life (Proverbs 18:21). This doesn't mean that just because you love people, you will always deliver hard words well. It also doesn't mean that just because someone loves you that they will receive hard words well. But saying hard things and loving the people we say them to are both necessary because God commands them both.

TRUTH & LOVE

We are commanded to "speak the truth in love" (Eph. 4:25). While truth and love are relative in the culture, they're not relative in God's Word. The Apostle John tells us, "By this we know that we love the children of God, when we love God and obey His commandments" (1 Jn. 5:2; cf. 2 Jn. 6). True love is defined by God's Word. We love God by obeying His commands, (Jn. 14:15) and we love others by allowing God's commands to govern everything we think, do, and say to them.

This certainly means we should say truthful words in a loving way. But in the church, we ought to do even more. We ought to trust one another because we love one another. Love is why we teach (1 Tim. 1:5), it motivates sacrificial living (Eph. 5:2), and it distinguishes us as God's children (Jn. 13:34–35). Truly, if a church lacks love, it has nothing (1 Cor. 13:1–3).

We also love by having hard conversations. We shouldn't enjoy rebuking others, but we should help them honor Jesus and experience the joy of obedience to him (Jn. 15:11). Admonishment shows love by exposing sins, addressing immaturity, or correcting error (cf. Rom. 15:14; 1 Cor. 4:14; Col. 3:16; 1 Thess. 5:12–14).

Paul publicly admonished Peter because his "conduct was not in step with the truth of the gospel" (Gal. 2:11–14). Paul's love for Peter, Barnabas, the Jews, the Gentiles, the church, and the name of Jesus compelled him to have a hard conversation. Love must do the same for us.

PAVING THE WAY

The old adage attributed to Richard Baxter rarely proves false, "If people can see you love them, you can say anything to them." What follows are five suggestions that display the kind of love that paves the way for hard conversations.

1. Pray together.

The Apostle Paul's relationships were marked by prayer.[81] God used prayer to endear churches to Paul and to knit Paul's heart with the churches. His many hard conversations were done through tears and with tender compassion (Acts 20:31; 2 Cor. 11:2). Though he was occasionally misunderstood, his prayerfulness proved his love for those churches (cf. 2 Cor; Gal.).

As we pray with and for fellow believers, God builds trust, love, empathy, and humility. Prayer guards us from self-righteousness and cultivates empathy toward others. Indeed, it's difficult to look down on people you constantly lift up in prayer. Having hard conversations is easier with people you've prayed for and with often because you both know your hope is ultimately in the Lord.

2. Welcome correction.

While our elders have shared hard words in recent weeks, we've also received hard words. Some members have shared their disappointment and frustration with the way we've handled some difficult issues. The conversations were heart-felt and humbling—and to be honest, they hurt. But we needed to have them. Our leadership had left some brothers and sisters wounded, and we needed to talk it out.

As pastors, we're not above correction. We should be models of receiving it. Jesus tells us in Matthew 7:1–5 that we must "first take the log out of [our] own eye" so we can see clearly to correct others. Pastors who are known for being humble, approachable, and willing to be corrected will be better received when we come to correct others.

3. Be scriptural.

When Scripture is central to the life of a church, it's natural for it to be central in personal conversations. If we're known for showing impartiality in our preaching, then we'll be trusted to show impartiality when engaging in conflict. If we're known for striving to live according to God's Word, then we'll be trusted when we call others to live it according to it as well.

When confronting a challenging issue, open the Bible. Don't use it as a bully's bat, but as a surgeon's scalpel. When everyone sits before the open Book to hear what God says, it brings humility and helps us discern the difference between sin and personal opinion. Prayerfully commit to letting God's voice be heard most clearly and let the light of his Word lead the way (Ps. 119:105).

4. Encourage often.

As a parent, it's easy for me to constantly critique my children. If I'm not careful, the only real conversations we have are when I'm frustrated with them.

---

81 Depending on how you count them, Paul mentions praying for churches in the New Testament 42 times.

Because of this, I strive to make encouragement prominent in our house. There's no perfect equation, but I hope to give three or four encouragements for every critique.

Similarly, pastors must often say hard things. But we must not *only* say hard things. We ought to "encourage one another every day, as long as it is called 'today,' that none of you may be hardened by the deceitfulness of sin" (Hebrews 3:13). The more we regularly encourage people, the easier it will be when we discuss something potentially discouraging.

There's nothing more encouraging than keeping Jesus central to your conversations. The aim of admonishment isn't to shame but serve one another by lifting our eyes to Jesus. Revisit his promised mercies that help in your weakness (Heb. 4:14–16). Remind one another that Jesus was condemned so they don't have to be (Rom. 8:1). Trust that he invites you because you are weak and that he will give grace to pursue peace (Matt. 11:28–30; 2 Cor. 12:9–10; Eph. 2:14).

5. *Keep trusting.*

Sometimes, hard conversations don't resolve smoothly. The split between Paul and Barnabas is a sobering reminder that disagreements can lead to undesired division (Acts 15:36–41). We must be careful not to evaluate the effectiveness of a hard conversation by someone's immediate response. Planted seeds often take time to sprout. If people choose to leave your church, then send them out in a way that lets them know they could always come back if they desired.

Several years ago, our elders received a surprising note from a former member. The sister had left our church three years prior after receiving what we sensed was warranted reproof. In her letter, she thanked us for saying hard things to her. She admitted that at the time she was offended and angered, but as time went on the Lord used the confrontation to help her grow. Today, she's walking with Jesus more faithfully. God used her humble response to encourage us.

You're not responsible for how someone responds to your reproof. But you are responsible for the way you love them. Hard conversations must happen, but make sure people have no doubt that your motivation is always, always, always love.

ABOUT THE AUTHOR

Garrett Kell is the lead pastor of Del Ray Baptist Church in Alexandria, Virginia.

Countering Conspiracy Theories Among Christians

Dan Darling

ell, that's what they want you to think," a friend insisted, with particular emphasis on the *they* and *want*, after the end of a long and fruitless argument about whether or not a group of secretive bankers was plotting in smoke-filled rooms to destroy the world. I tried, in vain, to convince him that Donald Trump's election, a natural disaster in Indonesia, and the rise of the price of plastics were not, in fact, tied to a central, evil, dark conspiracy.

You, too, probably have encountered a friend or family member convinced of a conspiracy. Perhaps you've had someone plead with you to "just watch this" or have had someone tell you, convincingly, "It's been proven!" and provide the web links to back it up.

Or maybe it's not a friend prone to believing in Sasquatch, UFOs, or that the world is flat; maybe you are the one who believes these things. If so, this might get awkward because I'm pretty skeptical of conspiracy theories. But hang with me, and let's at least agree to consider why Christians should be wise about the spread of information—especially information that might be dubious in nature or seems too good (or too nefarious) to be true.

Why We Want to Believe Conspiracy Theories

Conspiracy theories might get new life in the age of the internet, but as long as there has been the possibility of conspiracy, there have been conspiracy theories. What motivates otherwise rational human beings to suspend logic and indulge in ideas that to everyone else seem rather far-fetched?

Author and commentator Tom Nichols explains this in his book *The Death of Expertise*: "Conspiracy theories are . . . a way for people to give context and meaning to events that frighten them. . . . Without a coherent explanation for why terrible things happen to innocent people, they would have to accept such occurrences as nothing more than the random cruelty either of an uncaring universe or an incomprehensible deity."[1] For many, piecing together threads to form a narrative of blame brings a measure of comfort, a place to locate our rage or find some kind of grand purpose, even if nefarious, for the brokenness of our world.

Simply put, stitching together, for instance, disparate facts about a grassy knoll, a Russian mob, and Lyndon B. Johnson made it easier for America to cope with the sudden death of their beloved President Kennedy rather than accept that a lone fanatic named Lee Harvey Oswald assassinated the president in an attempt to be famous. Theologian and cultural commentator Albert Mohler says that such ideas "fill in all the gaps of what we don't know. When we can't connect why this happened and that happened, and why this person is here and that person is doing this, a conspiracy theory helps us to tie it all together. And that's very emotionally satisfying."[2] Of course, Christians, rather than rely on flimsy facts, should instead turn to the story the Bible tells of both Satan's conspiracy to corrupt the human race and defeat God and of Jesus' divine rescue that ushers in a new kingdom conspiracy of peace and love. The gospel is more emotionally satisfying, in the long run, than a rabbit trail of half-truths.

We venture down rabbit trails because, in a fallen world, there is actually the possibility of real conspiracy. To quote Mohler again, our Christian theology tells us "someone, somewhere is always plotting evil."[3] While most conspiracy theories are debunked, there are some that prove to be true. In the Bible we see tales of high-level corruption and cover-ups. Israel's greatest king, David, conspired to commit the murder of Bathsheba's husband and was exposed by Nathan the prophet (2 Sam. 12). Jesus himself was the victim of a nefarious plot, the ultimate inside job. His treasurer and close confidant, Judas Iscariot, betrayed Jesus and worked with religious and civil authorities to bring him to trial. History is dotted with examples of high-level mischief and secret plots of evil.

But why, today, in the modern era, have conspiracy theories found new life? I think there are three factors: the weakening of our key institutions, the democratization of information, and a lack of trust in the media.

First, we have to reckon with the way that institutions of power across our public life have profoundly failed us. Our political leaders have often been exposed to be dishonest and deceitful, with intricate networks of malice leading all the way to the highest offices. It's hard to pinpoint exactly when the decline in faith in American institutions began to wane, but scandals like Watergate, the sexual abuse scandals in Catholic and Protestant churches, financial meltdowns, and police misconduct have gradually eroded trust. Every institution in American society, it seems, has let us down. So, the reality of the possibility of scandal has bred in all of us the fear that everyone with power is corrupt. This is one reason we are easily duped into believing half-truths, untruths, and made-up stories.

This deficit of trust is also coming in an era where the flow of information is highly democratized. When I was a kid, news basically came in three forms: curated every morning in our three Chicago newspapers; at night from anchors with the big three news networks; and news radio stations. And if you wanted to find information about a specific person or place or thing, you'd thumb through your copy of the official *Encyclopedia Britannica* or you'd drive to the library and look through periodicals on microfilm.

Today, we seek out our own experts. We can read the first few results in Google (which probably ended up so near the top because they paid for the space), or scan articles posted by others on social media, or rely on email newsletters or podcasts. Before, the news was curated for us from the same few trusted sources; today we choose our news, based not only on ease but on ideological assumptions and biases.

This is not altogether bad. There are some real benefits to the deregulation of news. Stories that might have been ignored in a previous era because of certain biases of the mainstream media networks now get coverage. And yet the danger is that because we self-sort and find our information based on our political ideology, we can be extremely susceptible to believing what is untrue.

Senator Ben Sasse laments the corrosive impact of this self-sort on our democracy: "In the process, we've obliterated the gatekeepers who helped to ensure that information was important and reliable; we've erased the distinction between 'news' and 'opinion'; and we're losing the habits that could help us make calm, considered decisions. When it comes to consuming news, we're miles wide and an inch deep."[4]

Third, there is an impulse, especially among Christians, to distrust the media or any source of news. Too often mainstream journalists seem to have a bias against Christians in the way they cover religion or in the stories they emphasize. Too often media outlets highlight the craziest conservative, no matter how obscure, as an avatar for the whole movement while being hesitant to cover scandals that make liberals look bad. Still, we should admit that our willingness to entertain the outrageous and untrue is, in part, due to the fact that we want these stories to be true.

We not only are prone to believe the best or the worst about people about whom we want to believe the best or the worst, but we're prone to believing elaborate and often dangerous ideas that are at odds with the truth. This wanting stories to be true is what makes it so difficult to convince someone that a theory they think is so airtight is actually not at all true. Nichols explains this:

> Conspiracy theories, by contrast, are frustrating precisely because they are so intricate. Each rejoinder or contradiction only produces a more complicated theory. Conspiracy theorists manipulate all tangible evidence to fit their explanation, but worse, they will also point to the absence of evidence as even stronger confirmation. After all, what better sign of a really effective conspiracy is there than a complete lack of any trace that the conspiracy exists? Facts, the absence of facts, contradictory facts: everything is proof. Nothing can ever challenge the underlying belief.[5]

This kind of confirmation bias is why you can't argue your uncle or neighbor or Facebook sparring partner out of his ideas. It's why you can't convince a Holocaust denier or a flat-earther that they are wrong. Because in the cut-and-dried world of conspiracy, you are either with the conspirators as part of a cover-up or you are on the side of the angels who believe it.

Conspiracy theories also appeal to our vanity by giving us an exaggerated sense of being in the know, a kind of pseudo-omniscience that gives us the feeling of being in control. To know secrets is to have a knowledge that others don't possess. Carl Trueman, theologian and church historian, is right when he says that "conspiracy theories have an aesthetic appeal: they make us feel more important in the grand scheme of things than we are. If someone is going to all this trouble to con us into believing in something, then we have to be worth conning."[6]

Grand and improbable ideas not only help us find comfort but make us feel bigger when we feel small.

What Should Christians Do with Conspiracy Theories?

So maybe you've read this far and, like me, you roll your eyes at conspiracy theories. Or perhaps you are unconvinced and still think the moon landing was not in space but in a movie studio somewhere outside of Phoenix. "What's the big deal?" you might say. Does it matter if a few people indulge in far-out ideas? Who cares if our Thanksgiving meals are punctuated by wild tales of wicked deeds? Does it matter?

It does. For several reasons. First, even if speculating about the Kennedy assassination or sending an email that insists your most reviled politician is a tool of the Russian mafia seems harmless, as Christians, we should be committed to the truth. Paul urges the church at Philippi to think on "whatever is true [and] whatever is honorable" (Phil. 4:8).

Sadly, some followers of Jesus who claim to so boldly stand for truth are willing to create, spread, and post misinformation about people with whom they disagree or indulge fanatical tales about our ideological foes. Often we are the most gullible, the most willing to believe things that are not true. Perhaps this is why Paul often warned the early church against "silly myths" or fables (1 Tim. 1:4; 4:7). This is not just "going too far." Ed Stetzer, professor at Wheaton College and contributor to *Christianity Today*, says, "When you share such fake news and conspiracy theories, you are simply bearing false witness. That is a sin and it is time to repent."[7]

Christians need wisdom to discern between what is true and what is false. While we should hope that "unfruitful works of darkness" are exposed, we should avoid the rabbit trail of conspiracy theories because they both distract us from pursuing what is true and good and beautiful and because untruths damage the witness of the church. And while most crazy ideas from the internet are harmless, there are many conspiracy theories that, when spread, cause real harm. They spread misinformation, stoke fears, and can even lead to violence. A conspiracy about Hillary Clinton and a supposed trafficking ring once led a heavily armed young man to show up at a Washington, DC, pizza place.

Thankfully, he was stopped before he could commit real violence. But #pizzagate was not just harmless internet chatter. Nor is the growing movement of white nationalist ideology that is fueled by dangerous conspiracy theories that see people of color as societal problems. A young man from Plano, Texas, indulged these fantasies so much that he murdered twenty-two people in an El Paso Wal-Mart in cold blood. And the rise in Holocaust denial has often led to violence against Jewish people around the world.

These are extreme cases. But even when there is no violence involved, conspiracy theories damage reputations and hurt real people. Parents of children killed in mass shootings like Sandy Hook have had people stalk their property because they listened to conspiracy peddlers who insist their kids didn't really die but the entire tragedy was part of an elaborate "false flag" operation. Can you imagine the pain of not only losing a child to violence but also having someone track you down and harass you with wild accusations?

To indulge in these kinds of ideas is not only harmless. It's corrosive to the soul, damaging for our public witness, and it hurts neighbors we are called to love. In the church, this kind of fear-mongering conspiracy causes unnecessary division.

On several occasions I've had people approach me after a speaking engagement, insisting that the organization I previously worked for was part of a left-wing conspiracy funded by George Soros. Even though the funding sources and the budget was public record, and the trustees were voted on by the members of the denomination, work every year was an open parliamentary process, still the false rumors circulate. This was mostly annoying to me at this point, but it was distressing to know that thousands were being led to believe vile things about fellow brothers and sisters in Christ. Stetzer is right when he says, "spreading conspiracies and fake news directly violates Scripture's prohibition from bearing false witness against our neighbors. It devalues the name of Christ—whom we believe to be the very incarnation of truth—and it inflicts pain upon the people involved."[8]

We also need to examine the motivations that lead us to fall prey to such wild theories. If, as Mohler and Nichols asserted above, conspiracy theories give us a measure of comfort in troubling times, perhaps we are looking for peace where it cannot be ultimately found. Just before he urges the Philippian believers to think on what is true, Paul says that "the peace of God, which surpasses all understanding, will guard [our] hearts and minds in Christ Jesus" (Phil. 4:7). Conspiracy and intrigue gives us a sense of control, of knowing all things and being able to keep our fears in front of us. God calls us to a quiet peace, fueled by both trust in him and the mystery of faith.

Our connecting of unconnected dots is a cheap substitute for believing the ultimate story that explains the world. The Bible tells us evil and tragedy and sin find their root not in a smoke-filled room in Switzerland but with the "ruler of the power of the air, the spirit now working in the disobedient." Satan is the ultimate master conspirator and sin is the virus that has woven its way into every human heart. But we believers know that the man behind the curtain is on a leash, limited in power, and was defeated when Jesus uttered those agonizing words from a Roman cross: "It is finished" (John 19:30)!

The dots, for us, have been connected. And Jesus, the victor, has triumphed over the enemy. So while we participate with him in renewing and restoring the world, we can rejoice when evil is exposed without indulging dark and false fantasies.

The Mystery of Faith and the Seeking of Wisdom

This means we can live with mystery. Part of the reason we are so easily misled into conspiracy theories and silly myths is because we resist accepting the unknown and uncertain. And the easy reach of facts gives us the illusion of knowing all. Those quiet nights when I can't sleep, rather than rest and leave my finite thoughts to the Lord, I'm tempted to Google my problems away or find an explanation for what seems explainable. What leads us down these paths of irrational thought is both a denial of our own finite humanity and a forgetting of the humanness of others, especially those we think are caught up in some grand plot.

God doesn't want us to know everything. God's thoughts are higher and deeper and vaster than ours (Isa. 55:8–9), and this should give us comfort. He has the dots connected. He holds the worlds in his hands. He is sovereign even over the disparate strands of history and is gathering it all to himself. What great comfort.

In indulging far-out conspiracy theories, we also forget the finitude of those whom we assume are pulling the strings or plotting evil. There are some incredibly powerful world leaders and business executives and Hollywood personalities, but each of these is as human as we are. Sometimes in our fear, we assign them a power only God has. Carl Trueman reminds us, "nobody is that competent and powerful to pull them

[conspiracy theories] off. Even giant bureaucracies are made up of lots of small, incompetent units fighting petty turf wars."[9]

This isn't to say we should be naive about the possibility of evil. Cover-ups and malfeasance exist. But we should resist confirmation bias and pursue wisdom. The Bible tells us that the pursuit of wisdom is priceless (Prov. 8:11). Wisdom is the antidote to the kind of raw smorgasbord of data we have at our disposal in a digital age. This means we need to have a healthy skepticism toward the intake of information.

I'm amazed, frankly, at the way we are tempted to reject the authority of those who might have expertise and grant authority instead to our favorite sources online. Because our institutions have failed us, and experts, at times, get things wrong, we often reject the hard-won wisdom of people who have spent their lives accumulating the right kind of knowledge. Nichols says, "I fear we are witnessing the death of the ideal of expertise itself, a Google-fueled, Wikipedia-based, blog-sodden collapse of any division between professionals and laypeople, students and teachers, knowers and wonderers—in other words, between those of any achievement in an area and those with none at all."[10]

Nichols's book is incredibly helpful in recognizing our need for wisdom from experts who know more than we do. Because we can Google stuff, we think we are experts and often dismiss as

"elite" or "the establishment" those who have spent years pursuing actual useful knowledge in areas outside of our callings. Thinking on what is true requires us to lean on the knowledge of experts, to understand our own intellectual limitations, and to resist the lie that says we can be all-knowing.

It's actually quite arrogant for me to assume that, for example, a doctor who has studied in medical school for years knows less about my health than some random Google search. Or that my friend who works in pediatric infectious disease at a university research hospital, an elder in his church, and committed Christian brother, knows less about the validity of vaccinations for my children than I do. It's even more foolish to trust one person on the internet more than the shared knowledge of medical professionals who study these things for a living. The Bible tells us wisdom is often found, not in finding ideas that confirm our fears or appeal to what we already believe or want to be true, but in a multitude, a community of wisdom (Prov. 11:14).

And so, to guard against falling for bad ideas, conspiracy theories, or false information, we should cultivate the humility of asking, seeking, and tempering our certainties with humility. We don't know everything. We are not experts at everything. A life of faith that loves God with all of our minds requires us to seek the truth, reject what isn't true, and hold our biases loosely in order to let God transform and renew us (Rom. 12:2).

As much as we affirm that embracing truth leads to human flourishing, we have to admit that spreading falsehoods leads to human brokenness. And we should do our part to stop misinformation. This doesn't mean we have to be the annoying person on Facebook always correcting minor facts, but we should be hesitant to share or spread anything we don't know to be true and, in our circles of influence, should cultivate healthy habits of information consumption. This means self-curating what knowledge we take in by reading from diverse media outlets, not merely ones whose ideological biases conform to ours. And we should resist the pull toward conspiracy, half-truths, and tabloid-style clickbait that is harmful for a civil society.

In doing so, we may not convince our conspiracy-loving uncle at Thanksgiving, but our pursuit of truth can set an example that might push back against lies and our public witness might point people to the end of our pursuit of knowledge: Jesus, the wisdom of God.

NOTES

1. Tom Nichols, *The Death of Expertise: The Campaign Against Established Knowledge and Why It Matters* (New York: Oxford University Press, 2017), 58.
2. Albert Mohler, "How Should Christians Respond to Conspiracy Theories?" Ask Anything Live, 2019, https://www.youtube.com/watch?v=EiGJJeTyye0.
3. Ibid.
4. Ben Sasse, *Them: Why We Hate Each Other—and How to Heal* (New York: St. Martin's Press, 2018), 79.
5. Nichols, *The Death of Expertise*, 55.
6. As quoted by Justin Taylor, "The Vanity of Conspiracy Theories and the Banality of Real Evil," The Gospel Coalition (blog), accessed September 6, 2019, https://www.thegospelcoalition.org/blogs/justin-taylor/the-vanity-of-conspiracy-theories-and-the-banality-of-real-evil/.
7. Ed Stetzer, "Christians, Repent (Yes, Repent) of Spreading Conspiracy Theories and Fake News—It's Bearing False Witness," *The Exchange*, accessed September 6, 2019, https://www.christianitytoday.com/edstetzer/2017/may/christians-repent-conspiracy-theory-fake-news.html.
8. Ibid.
9. As quoted in Taylor, "The Vanity of Conspiracy Theories and the Banality of Real Evil."
10. Nichols, *The Death of Expertise*.

EDITOR'S NOTE

A Special Thanks to B&H for permission to reprint this adaptation of chapter 7 of Dan Darling's A Way With Words: Using our Online Conversations for Good (Nashville, TN: B&H, 2020)

DANIEL DARLING

Daniel Darling is the Senior Vice President for Communications at NRB (National Religious Broadcasters)

"Sir, This Is a Local Church"—Or, How an Absurdist Meme about a Roast Beef Shop Might Help Heal Our Church

Alex Duke

I wonder if you're familiar with the "Sir, this is an Arby's" meme. Let me illustrate it for you:

Person A [with aggressive aggravation]: Can you believe it? The other day, I heard someone refer to the *book* of Genesis. Surely you KNOW that Genesis is not just "a book," but the first part of the Pentateuch, and the Pentateuch is *a five-fold book*, not five *books*. Do you know what the first word is in Exodus, Leviticus, Numbers, and Deuteronomy? It's *and*. BOOM. What did Jesus call the Torah? "The *book* of Moses." Not the *books* of Moses.

Person B [laconically]: Sir, this is an Arby's.

That's it. That's the joke. The point of the punchline is simple: Arby's isn't the place for unhinged ramblings about the Torah, and an Arby's cashier is only there to take your order and ask if you want horseradish or not.

As the managing editor of 9Marks, it's kind of my job to trawl the Christian Internet. Please notice I said to *trawl*, as in "to sift through," not to *troll*, as in "to be a jerk." Over the past few months of quarantine and political unrest, I've thought about this Arby's meme a lot—partly because I tend to diffuse tense and fractious situations with humor, and partly because this meme offers an absurdist rendition of what's going on in churches across the world.

Let me explain. While I'm trawling, lots of folks are trolling. They're angry, incredulous, fed-up, distraught, galled. About what? The manipulation of COVID-19 stats. The hypocrisy of state-celebrated protests. The uselessness of masks. Police brutality. Black-on-black crime. Vice President Biden's flaws or peccadillos. President Trump's flaws or peccadillos. How 9Marks is too "woke." How John MacArthur has blood on his hands. How closing a church is cowardice. How opening a church is courage.

Worse than trolling on Twitter is how they pillory their pastor. Some are mad because their pastors haven't done enough. *How could you stand idly by when racial injustice is everywhere?* Others are mad because their pastors have done too much. *How could you say that in your pastoral prayer? You don't know the facts!?*

Many church members are happy and content. But many are aggrieved.

1. Some are *legalists*. They *demand* that their pastor use his platform to decry everything they themselves want to decry. They want to use him to boost and legitimate their personal opinions.

2. Some are *conversationalists*. They want their pastor to broker conversations within the church about various issues of the day. When their pastor elects *not* to host that forum or teach that Sunday School class or start that reading group, they can be tempted to

assume the worst—he doesn't care; he's privileging of one view over another.

3. Finally, some—perhaps most—are *quietists*. They say nothing at all, yet they silently *wonder* why the pastor isn't saying anything either—about the issues themselves, or about the way other members talk about the issues online. Because of this, they're tempted toward distrust. Some of course appreciate their pastor's silence. After all, they used to go to churches that lurched after every headline like a cat after a laser pointer. It was fun for a while, but eventually the whole exercise became tiring and even a bit sad.

"BROTHER / SISTER, THIS IS AN ARBY'S"

So what do we do? How do we respond to all three types and more?

I have an idea. It's inspired by my beloved meme, and I think it would work in nearly every situation. Rather simply, we can say, "Brother . . . sister, this is a local church."

The point of the punchline is simple: your church isn't the place for such activity, and your pastor isn't the one who should celebrate all your political inclinations, setting them alongside God's Word. Helping your people understand "This is a church" will release some of the pressure and make our churches happier places.

As my friend Adam Sinnett recently wrote:

So, while there are many things the church *could* do, what it *must* do is faithfully proclaim the gospel and cultivate worship-full disciples as God's new humanity in Jesus. While the church cares deeply about politics, it is not a partisan organization. While the church cares deeply about justice, it is not a social justice organization. While the church cares deeply about current events, it is not a news organization which offers ongoing cultural commentary. While the church cares deeply about virtue, it is not responsible to signal its virtue to merely appease the culture.

The church is a local expression of God's new, diverse, redeemed people with a specific purpose: to faithfully proclaim the gospel and cultivate worship-full disciples for God's glory. While there are many things we *could* do, this is what we *must* do. This is the heart beat of every faith-filled, Bible-saturated, Spirit-dependent, God-centered, Christ-satisfied local church. This is where our primary energies should be directed. This is what we should expect from a healthy local church, whether gathered or scattered.

I believe he's right. To that end, and with some aid from the book of Ephesians, here are three things you want your members to know for the sake of our gospel unity in politically divisive times.

First and foremost, a church is *a people*.

And let me tell you the most important thing about these people: God chose them in love before the foundation of the world. They've been redeemed by the blood of Christ and therefore stand holy and blameless before a holy and righteous God. These chosen-and-redeemed ones have heard the gospel, recognized it as the word of truth, and believed it (Eph. 1:1–14).

It's absolutely vital that we remember this. A church isn't an agenda-setting or landscape-altering religious think tank. It's a redeemed people. It's the culmination of an eternally purposed Trinitarian plan that centers on the glory and wisdom and grace of the Godhead displayed in the redemption not of ideas, but of individuals.

So the next time you're tempted to rail against or assume the worst of another Christian—whether in your church or elsewhere—just remember: you're blood brothers. The same blood that bought you bought them, the same blood that made the forgiveness of your trespasses possible made their forgiveness of their trespasses possible, the same blood that made you holy and blameless made them holy and blameless. You're sealed siblings, awaiting the same glorious inheritance. Might dwelling on this change how we address our disagreements, even about the important stuff?

So brothers and sisters, remember: *this is a local church.*

Second, a church is not a war-zone, but *an already-won territory of peace.*

In Ephesians 2:1–10, Paul explains how individual Christians are saved—by grace, through faith, not by works, so that no one may boast. We are his workmanship (2:10). Then he goes on to explain what kind of work he's building. If Ephesians 2:1–10 describes the individual bricks, then Ephesians 2:11–22 describes the *building*—and it's a spectacular one. Consider:

- *Christ* has brought us near (v. 13).
- *He* is our peace (v. 14).
- *He* has created *in himself* one new man, where there were once two (v. 15).
- Where there was once hostility, *he* has made possible peace and reconciliation (v. 15–16)
- *He* has made us fellow citizens of a new territory: the household of God. This house is built on a foundation of true gospel doctrine, and its cornerstone is Christ himself (v. 19–20).
- This house Jesus is building is growing into a holy temple, where God dwells with man by the Spirit (v. 21–22).

Now, think about the person in your church whose opinions make you the most angry—you know, that guy or gal who spouts off about this or that and in the process assumes everyone who doesn't agree with them is not only stupid but unspiritual. Is your blood boiling yet? A little warm around the collar? Then look at these bullet points again. Yes, Paul is describing the healed rift between Jews and Gentile, but his words also apply to you and that guy. Yep, *that* guy.

Why did our Triune God do all this? Because he's had an eternal purpose since eternity past (3:11). He had a mystery, yet he hid it and hid it and hid it—that is, until the Light of the world came to bring it to light (3:9). What is this mystery now-revealed? It's the church as the people of God! It's *your* church that will make known to all heavenly rulers and authorities God's manifold wisdom.

Brothers and sisters, *this is a local church.*

Third, a church's primary assailants are supernatural, not personal—and its primary weapons are spiritual, not political.

Paul ends his letter to the Ephesians by telling them to get ready for war. Now *that* sounds like a message fit for 2020. But did you notice how he describes the enemy?

> Put on the whole armor of God, that you may be able to stand against the schemes of the devil. For we do not wrestle against flesh and blood, but against the rulers, against the authorities, against the cosmic powers over this present darkness, against the spiritual forces of evil in the heavenly places. (Eph. 6:11–12)

Our greatest enemy in an election year is our greatest enemy in a non-election year. Our greatest enemy in a democracy is our greatest enemy in a dictatorship. That enemy is not *the other*, but the Adversary. He's not an elephant or a donkey, but a lion on the prowl, looking for someone to devour.

But here's where it gets tricky though. Some Christians think the Republican Party's support of President Trump is demonic; others think that the Democratic Party's support of abortion is demonic. What do we do about this?

We ought to remember precisely what Paul tells us to remember: that we're *not* warring against flesh and blood. Our brothers and sisters and Christ might be misguided or naive or even worse—but they're decidedly *not* our adversaries. Satan is. And whatever machinations he's got going on in the halls of government are far less relevant than whatever he's up to in the pews of your church.

I'm not sure exactly what the devil thinks of the election, but I know he cares immensely that Christians hate the people they're supposed to love. Because when we do, we dim our witness to the watching world

(Eph. 3:10). We rip out the beating evangelistic heart that's supposed to typify every healthy local church: its members' love for one another (John 13:35).

For some, the world seems to have lost its ever-loving mind recently. For others, the world has ignored an endemic sickness for too long and is finally taking its medicine—yes, we're gagging as the Robitussin goes down, but we know it's good for us.

How are Christians supposed to respond? Consider Luke 21. While I can't explain everything in this chapter in this article, Jesus' words about the posture of his people are straightforward:

> "And when you hear of wars and tumults, do not be terrified, for these things must first take place, but the end will not be at once." Then he said to them, "Nation will rise against nation, and kingdom against kingdom. There will be great earthquakes, and in various places famines and pestilences. And there will be terrors and great signs from heaven. (Luke 21:9–12)

Alright, that's the confusing part. But here's where it gets simple. Before all this weird and wild stuff happens:

> They will lay their hands on you and persecute you, delivering you up to the synagogues and prisons, and you will be brought before kings and governors for my name's sake. This will be your opportunity to bear witness. Settle it therefore in your minds not to meditate beforehand how to answer, for I will give you a mouth and wisdom, which none of your adversaries will be able to withstand or contradict. You will be delivered up even by parents and brothers and relatives and friends, and some of you they will put to death. You will be hated by all for my name's sake. But not a hair of your head will perish. By your endurance you will gain your lives. (vv. 12–19)

Did you catch it? All this craziness, Jesus says, will be our *opportunity to bear witness*. How? By enduring. By showing solidarity over and against even the deepest worldly relationships: parents, siblings, relatives, and friends. By trusting that the Lord will provide us with everything we need—that even if we die, we'll never perish.

We need to remember who our enemies are. We also need to remember the weapons Jesus authorizes us to use. In Luke 21, Jesus ends his ominous predictions with an exhortation. In short: stay alert and pray (21:36). That's what we should do.

We want to do more, of course. We want to fight fire with, well, fire. We see people rejecting Jesus so we wonder, like James and John in Luke 9, "Lord, do you want us to tell fire to come down from heaven and consume them?" In these regrettable moment, I suspect Jesus responds to us as he did to them: he turns around and rebukes us.

Ephesians 6 sounds a similar note. Paul tells us to keep alert and to pray (6:18–19). He tells the church to take up the *armor* of God—not to unleash the *arsenal* of God. We're given details of a defensive wardrobe, not an offensive war-chest. But there is, of course, one exception: the sword of the Spirit which is the word of God (6:17).

A few implications from this: first, Christians ought to be marked by their alertness and their prayerfulness. We ought to pay attention to our world—not so that we can grouse at the latest idiocy or injustice, but so that our prayers will be full of both informed hopefulness and particular concern.

Second, when we go on the offensive, we must only do so when we're prayed-up and when we're able to specifically and unambiguously apply the Word of God. Put another way: don't go on the offensive about your opinions.

Our churches should be the first place we see Isaiah 2 coming to fruition:

> It shall come to pass in the latter days
>> that the mountain of the house of the Lord
> shall be established as the highest of the mountains,
>> and shall be lifted up above the hills;
> and all the nations shall flow to it,
>> and many peoples shall come, and say:

"Come, let us go up to the mountain of the Lord,
    to the house of the God of Jacob,
that he may teach us his ways
    and that we may walk in his paths."
For out of Zion shall go forth the law,
and the word of the Lord from Jerusalem.
He shall judge between the nations,
    and shall decide disputes for many peoples;
and they shall beat their swords into plowshares,
and their spears into pruning hooks;
nation shall not lift up sword against nation,
    neither shall they learn war anymore.

Brothers and sisters, remember: *this is a local church.*

ABOUT THE AUTHOR

Alex Duke is the editorial manager for 9Marks.

Should You Be a Political Activist?

Brian Davis

Should you be a political activist?

Maybe. Maybe not. While I think that's a good question to think about (with others and an open Bible), I am more interested that there is freedom given for godly saints to answer that question in different ways. I think Christian charity should make more room for different good responses to that question. We must enlarge our view of faithfulness.

WHAT'S REQUIRED OF EVERY CHRISTIAN

Let's start with some of what's required of every Christian.

Christ calls all of us to be the salt and light (Matt. 5:13–14). All of us, therefore, should have a seasoning, preserving, and illuminating influence in this dark and perverse generation. We cannot transform the world into something salvageable (1 Cor. 7:31), but we can influence the world for good as recipients of God's salvation and "adorn the doctrine of God our Savior" (Titus 2:10). We ought to work to diminish participation in sin, expose the existence of sin, proclaim that Christ is Savior and Lord, and supply a heavenly contrast that attracts attention to our Lord and his gospel.

Further, Scripture commands all of us to pray for the improvement of our societies and those who lead them:

> First of all, then, I urge that supplications, prayers, intercessions, and thanksgivings be made for all people, for kings and all who are in high positions, that we may lead a peaceful and quiet life, godly and dignified in every way. This is good, and it is pleasing in the sight of God our Savior, who desires all people to be saved and to come to the knowledge of the truth. (1 Tim. 2:1-4)

Such prayers are "good," because they lead to good outcomes: peaceful and quiet lives which allow people to come to knowledge of the truth. And, historically, Christians have understood that what is *prayed for* in private is to be *labored for* in public. We are not only to earnestly make "good prayers", but also be a people "zealous for good works" (Titus 2:14).

If you're a Christian, you're called to enthusiastically labor for good works. A fallen and sinful world is filled with opportunities to do good as God's people so that we can proclaim the excellencies of him who calls from darkness to marvelous light. And to all of this, the church says, "Amen!"

A VAST UNIVERSE OF GOOD WORKS TO DO

These opportunities to do good should be a point of celebration, however they are also a place of contention. We pit one good work against another, or we require every other Christian to take up the same good work that we are most passionate about ourselves.

When we do this, we end up shrinking faithfulness to Jesus into our smaller expressions of it.

Yet there is a vast universe of good works to do. There are multiple courses of action that are equally faithful to God. The Bible does not offer a list of all the good works because there are countless ways this will play out in each Christian's life.

Some may frequently protest; others may never participate in one.

Some may vote; others may not vote at all.

Some might become an activist who labors to be an agent of change in society; others may focus their attention on their own affairs and seek to honor Christ in the quiet confines of their day-to-day lives.

Some will go out; some will stay put.

Some are prone to mourn in compassion, while others are prone to rejoice in hope.

Some will tweet much, some will tweet little, and some will not tweet at all!

Some will believe that much can change in the present world through faithful labor; some will believe that much won't change in a fallen world and so they'll spend their energies in what they deem more fruitful.

Some will, "Answer not a fool according to his folly, lest you be like him yourself" (Prov. 26:4); others will "Answer a fool according to his folly, lest he be wise in his own eyes" (Prov. 26:5)!

All of it is faithfulness. There is a time and a season for everything (Eccl. 3:1-8).

There's much that we all *must* do. We all *must* pray consistently with the shape of our Lord's agenda (Mt. 6:7–13); we all *must* abstain from every form of evil (1 Thess 5:22); we all *must* be zealous for good works (Titus 2:14); we all *must* repent and believe the gospel (Mk. 1:15) we all *must* obey all of Christ's commands (Matt. 28:20)!

But this doesn't mean that our obedience is going to be utterly identical. Sure, there are many ways it should be identical (like our belief in the gospel), but there are many, *many* ways it should look beautifully diverse (like our efforts to adorn the gospel).

CHARITY & FREEDOM

What's often missing in our calls to action is *charity* and *freedom*. We need more charity that says, "Even though you don't agree with me or take up the cause I am passionate about—I still welcome you and affirm you as my family in Christ."

We also need to give more freedom for different believers to do different things—things consistent with Scripture—and still be regarded as equally faithful to the Lord. You don't have to be an activist to love Jesus. You don't have to march in protests to be faithful to God. You certainly *can* do those things to the glory of God, but you don't *have* to do those things to give glory to God.

Perhaps you are not an activist, but you should be! Or perhaps you *are* an activist, and you shouldn't be. Let everyone be convinced in his own mind, and let everyone be careful not to judge what his brother has concluded in his. Some will partake as unto the Lord, and some will abstain as unto the Lord. God welcomes both—and so too, should we (see Romans 14).

It's really quite simple: if the only way to be faithful to Jesus is *your* way, then you have lost Jesus. Disciples are called to observe Jesus' commandments, not yours.

We all must be extremely careful not to teach as doctrines the commandments of men (Mark 7:7). Just because you have a good idea to honor the Lord doesn't mean I am required by God to participate with you. Believers don't "cancel" each other due to matters of conscience, but rather we extend charity to each other where we disagree. We need to make room for each other in Christ, for God has made room for us all.

WHAT GOD WILL RECOGNIZE ON JUDGMENT DAY

We tend to think God prefers lives full of big events and epic efforts of faithfulness. Some insist that loud and big solutions are the only faithful way forward, that anything short of a revolution is unacceptable. But Jesus hasn't called us *all* to revolutionize our governments or to change *all* the unjust policies of our communities. Perhaps some of his people will be used by him to bring about dramatic change, and praise God if so!

But most Christians cannot effect change on that level and will not affect change on that level. Often, we are not providentially given access to make such adjustments. Sometimes we will have good desires without particular outlets for such good works. Gal. 6:10 says, "as we have opportunity—do good to everyone", and oftentimes we do not have opportunities to make world shifting changes. While we can certainly be bright influences in a crooked and dark world, we will always live in an evil age until Christ makes all things new (Rom. 8:19).

Therefore, let's keep in the forefront of our minds what Jesus will recognize at the final Judgment. His words stand out with refreshing simplicity in a world that seems fixated on large and loud responses. He doesn't want us to miss the many opportunities he has given to be faithful to him by overlooking the small things. Here's what Jesus says:

> The King will say to those on his right, "Come, you who are blessed by my Father, inherit the kingdom prepared for you from the foundation of the world. For I was hungry and you gave me food, I was thirsty and you gave me drink, I was a stranger and you welcomed me, I was naked and you clothed me, I was sick and you visited me, I was in prison and you came to me." Then the righteous will answer him, saying, "Lord, when did we see you hungry and feed you, or thirsty and give you drink? And when did we see you a stranger and welcome you, or naked and clothe you? And when did we see you sick or in prison and visit you?" And the King will answer them, "Truly, I say to you, as you did it to one of the least of these my brothers, you did it to me." Matt 25:34-40

Jesus will bring up the good works that people may not have noticed. He will honor the religion and regard the good works that many saints overlooked. It's significant to note that what Jesus recalled, the righteous didn't even remember! To be sure, there are louder, more easily noticed obediences. But quiet obediences are equally noticed by God. Just because someone is living a quiet life doesn't mean that *that* life isn't godly and dignified in every way.

DON'T SHRINK FAITHFULNESS

So as we seek to stir up one another to love and good works, let's be careful not to shrink what faithfulness is.

Let's make room for different burdens in the brethren.

Let's encourage one another to pursue diverse good works throughout the church.

And let's remember that Jesus measures differently than we do. That small obedience from a saint that we might conclude is an insufficient expression of faithfulness, Jesus may well regard as more than enough.

ABOUT THE AUTHOR

Brian Davis lives in Philadelphia with his wife, Sonia, and their two sons, Spurgeon and Sibbes. He is part of the church planting team for Risen Christ Fellowship.

What Makes A Vote Moral or Immoral? The Ethics of Voting

Jonathan
Leeman

Jonathan
Leeman

AUTHOR'S NOTE

Two versions of the same article are below. The second one is 8000 words. I wrote it first. I commend it to anyone who wants to think through the ethics of voting slowly and carefully, with a lot of the nuances and "what ifs" some of us want. The shorter one clocks in at 2400 words for anyone in a bit more of a hurry. This tactic—writing the longer then shorter version—is one I have often used in my writing career. Both have their purposes, perhaps most of all the development of my own thinking on a topic!

—SHORT VERSION—

In this article I'm not going to tell you how to vote in the next election. I'm not going to tell you what makes for a good or wise vote. I'm even not going to offer my full moral evaluation of the upcoming 2020 elections in the United States.

Rather, my goal is merely to offer nine principles that will help you determine for yourself whether a given vote is morally better or worse or at least morally permissible. God has given you the Bible and pastors like me to offer you principles. Yet he has also given you a conscience and created you to make these kinds of moral judgments.

Further, I think I would be pastorally overstepping were I to tell you how I think you positively *should* vote, assuming there is more than one permissible option (which includes not voting, voting for a third party, writing in a candidate, or even civil disobedience if you live in a country with compulsory voting). At most, I think a pastor can, from time to time, warn you against paths you should *not* take. Seldom if ever should he tell you which path you *should* take, assuming that doing so closes down other morally permissible paths.

NINE PRINCIPLES

The nine principles build cumulatively, with the first being most foundational and the ninth incorporating everything.

1. Your vote bears moral weight by virtue of a chain of causation.

When you vote in a democratic system, you're actually participating in the role of the "governing authorities" that Paul and Peter describe. Your job is to align your objectives with the purposes which God gives to the government in Scriptures, such as "punish[ing] those who do evil and praise[ing] those who do good" (1 Peter 2:13–14; see also, Gen. 9:5–6; Rom. 13:1–7; etc.).

Therefore, your vote requires you to make a moral evaluation about what's good and what's evil, or wise and unwise (see Prov. 8:15–16), and then to act on behalf of your evaluation. You are morally responsible for this evaluation and act of judgment.

Suppose then candidate Jack says he believes in positions *a, b, c, d,* and *e,* while candidate Jill supports issues *l, m, n, o,* and *p.* When I cast a ballot for

"

Jack, I am giving Jack the *agency*—that is, the power or ability—he needs for turning *a, b, c, d,* and *e* into law over and against *l, m, n, o,* and *p.* If Jack is elected and succeeds in writing *a, b, c, d,* and *e* into law, I become morally culpable for those laws, at least in some measure, by the simple formula of cause and effect with my vote as the first cause. Our votes create the requisite agency. We're handing Jack or Jill the sword of state.

2. With regard to what a vote *does*, your motives don't matter (but see point 8).

Suppose you believe issue *e* is wicked, yet vote for Jack because you really care about *a, b, c,* and *d.* Still, you cannot discount what your vote *does.* It gives Jack agency to pursue *a, b, c, d,* and *e,* and you remain morally responsible for that. There's no way to absolve yourself of moral responsibility for the one thing you don't like and to keep it for the four things you do like. Voting ballots are dumb. They cannot discern your motives. The moral chain of causation remains. Recall, furthermore, that Scripture acknowledges a category for "unintentional sin" (Lev. 4).

3. There's a distinction between morally permissible laws and immoral laws which is crucial to our moral evaluations.

Some laws or actions promised by a candidate, in and of themselves, are morally permissible, even if they eventually prove to have unjust outcomes. For instance, think of laws establishing the tax rate at *x* percent, or to establish an immigration quota at *y* people per year, or to incarcerate a person for *z* years for possessing an illegal drug.

Other laws, by their very nature, are always unjust (see Is. 10:1–2). So it is, for instance, with laws establishing race-based slavery, segregation, or discriminatory mortgage-lending practices. And so it is with laws establishing abortion.

Our posture toward morally permissible laws with bad or unjust outcomes should be different than our posture toward morally unjust laws. With morally permissible laws, we can talk about "reducing the bad outcomes," even while continuing to affirm the moral permissibility of a law. Not so with inherently unjust laws. The goal with unjust laws must be to overturn them, plain and simple, lest our ongoing support affirm what's inherently unjust (see Rom. 1:32). What sense would it make to support a pro-slavery senator while seeking to reduce the number of slaves?

Now, realpolitik considerations sometimes involve compromises. Half a loaf is better than no loaf, they say. Still, even as we accept halfway measures for the sake of reducing bad outcomes, our overall goal and strategy must remain overturning the unjust law.

4. The character of a candidate matters by the same chain of moral causation described in point 1.

Does the character of a candidate matter to the ethical significance of a vote? Yes, and it does by the same chain of moral causation described above, only now culpability transfers not through issues like *a, b, c, d,* and *e,* but through the person him or herself. If I choose a babysitter for my children whom I know has poor character, or a landlord for the apartment building I own whom I know has poor character, or a treasurer for my church whom I know has poor character, I become at least partially complicit in any bad decisions each of these individuals make.

Jesus tells us that, "Every good tree produces good fruit, but a bad tree produces bad fruit" (Matt. 7:17). If I knowingly plant a bad tree in my garden, is just the tree then responsible for the basket of bad fruit which my children carry inside? Am I not responsible, too?

A leader's character and behavior teaches and even authorizes what's morally acceptable within that leader's domain. Suppose a baseball coach has a pattern of telling racist jokes. By doing so, he's teaching his players that racist jokes are acceptable. In a sense, he's even authorizing them to sit in the dugout and make such jokes among each other. He's creating some space in their conscience for such activity, even if other authorities in their lives condemn racist jokes. In other words, character has a very real and tangible effect on a body politic that's analogous to passing a law. It's like the passing of an informal and unspoken law supporting those things, which people will notice and follow (see 1 Tim. 4:16). A leader's life is powerful.

Suppose then you knowingly hire this baseball coach who makes racist jokes. Do you not risk becoming at least somewhat complicit in his racism? If so, might not the same principle apply to voting for a dishonest and unvirtuous candidate?

5. Saying "But Democracy!" doesn't sanctify your vote.

People say, surely there's *always* a morally righteous choice. That's true, but the Bible never guarantees one of the two major candidates in an American election is a righteous choice. Maybe the righteous choice is not voting or writing in a candidate (see principle 7 below). Let's make sure we're not sacralizing democracy.

6. There are a number of rocks on the scale, but some rocks are heavier than others.

Two principles are bound up in this point, and we need to pay attention to both simultaneously. On the one hand, a just government must attend to a multitude of issues—the economy, foreign policy, national defense, criminal justice, healthcare, various social issues, and more. There are a number of rocks on the moral scales that Lady Justice must weigh. On the other hand, some rocks are heavier than others (Matt. 23:23). They're more morally significant.

Thinking ethically about voting means accounting for more than one rock, but it also means acknowledging that some rocks are heavier than others.

A related point here concerns the question of "one-issue voting." Can one issue disqualify a candidate? Hopefully every Christian would say that a pro-stealing, or pro-pedophilia, or pro-slavery candidate is disqualified, no matter how good he or she is on other issues. I wish everyone would arrive at this conclusion on abortion.

Also, can bad character disqualify a candidate, potentially outweighing the other rocks on the scale? If what we said above is true—that bad authorizes and creates moral space for immoral activity—it's hard to see how bad character cannot disqualify someone.

Imagine how radically the political landscape would change if every Christian in the United States embraced the last two paragraphs. Some will call this idealism, which might be a fair critique if "idealism" means acting on principles, not outcomes. That, too, is something you must weigh: pure principles vs. realistic outcomes. My recommendation is to weigh these things preparing yourself for the Lord's final judgment.

7. Is it morally permissible to not vote or to vote for a candidate that is certain to lose? It depends.

Ordinarily, I believe it's morally better to vote than not to vote. God has given us a stewardship with the blessing of a vote, and we don't want to be like the servant who buried his talent in the ground. Why should we vote? For the sake of love of neighbor and justice.

That said, nowhere does the Bible say a person must pursue love and justice *by* voting. Therefore, if a person is convinced in his conscience that he'd be sinning by voting for Jack and Jill both, I would say he shouldn't vote for either, so long as he is fully convinced in his mind (see Rom. 14:5).

Perhaps slightly better than abstaining from voting is to vote for a candidate that one's conscience can accept, even if that candidate is certain to lose, because you're still participating in the election process and formally registering what you believe is right and just.

8. With regard to church membership, your motives matter.

Moral evaluation among Christians operates in two gears. Gear 1: our determination of right and wrong. Gear 2: our determination of wrongs that, apart from repentance, require excommunication or removal from membership in the church. What's key here is that not every moral evaluation in Gear 1 will downshift into Gear 2.

You might be personally convicted that a certain vote is probably sin (Gear 1), but for any number of reasons decide that it's not a sin for which you would recommend excommunication.

For instance, I believe it's ordinarily a sin to vote for a pro-choice candidate, by virtue of principles 1, 2, and 6 above (Gear 1). Furthermore, if someone was voting for the pro-choice candidate *because* of his or her support for abortion, I would probably recommend excommunication (Gear 2). Christians absolutely must not support abortion.

Suppose, however, a fellow church member told you she was voting for the pro-choice candidate *in spite of* the candidate's view on abortion. She hates abortion, yet she says she's unconvinced the pro-life party is actually pro-life. She cares about other issues, too, and she sees other strategic considerations in play (see principle 9 below). I would still affirm my own conviction that she was probably sinning for her support of that candidate (as an unintentional instance of Romans 1:32), and I would want to persuade her otherwise. But I would still affirm my willingness to come to the Lord's Table with her.

In short, a fellow Christian's motives do make a difference, *at least in terms of how I would relate to someone as a fellow Christian.* And here the difference between *because of* and *in spite of* is meaningful.

Does this mean Christians should accept any potential vote so long as the person says they're voting for a candidate *in spite of* the evil aims of the candidate? No. When the occasion comes that a party exists almost exclusively for the purpose of wickedness, when a particular evil becomes an entity's *raison d'etre*, then at that point churches should consider excommunication for party membership or support. For instance, it's difficult to know how someone could vote for the KKK *in spite of* its racism and not *because of* its racism. The KKK exists expressly for the purpose of racism. To be sure, there's no mathematically precise way to determine when that moment for a major party comes. For the Nazi Party, that moment arguably came in 1934 with the Barmen Declaration. Yet every instance involves a judgment call, and every church, as led by its elders, needs to ask the Lord for wisdom, moral clarity, and courage to make that judgment.

9. In the final analysis, ethically evaluating our votes involves *both* moral principles *and* strategic calculations.

We need to view any given vote within the larger and highly elaborate *game* of democratic governance. A game, of course, consists of several periods and many moves. Plus, you don't judge the success or failure of a game by any one period or move. You judge each move by how it contributes to the outcome of the whole game. And the game of politics transpires over multiple election cycles.

If the first principle above laid the foundation upon which the rest of the principles built, this last principle is the earthquake that shakes the building and makes the whole structure of our moral evaluation look a little less sturdy.

For instance, suppose a friend tells you he intends to vote for candidate Jack who supports something you both believe is wrong. Yet due to a host of realpolitik considerations, he believes voting for Jack is a better long-term strategy for your shared cause. It's hypothetically possible he's right, though you seriously doubt it. How then do we morally evaluate his action? You might still warn him he's probably sinning in his vote, but also affirm that you're not ready to break fellowship with him because he's seeking a good end.

What's crucial, however, is that his overall goal must be to overturn the intrinsically unjust law, as in principle 3 above. He cannot wave off the injustice and say, "Well, it's never going to change. I might as well focus on other things." His heart would need to cry out against the injustice. In short, a smidgeon of flexibility might be permitted only at the tactical level, not at the level of what his heart *and* actions must be set against.

CONCLUSION

How then should you ethically evaluate the different candidates on offer in the next election? That hard work is now over to you.

Look over these principles again. Supply any additional ones that you think might be missing. Educate yourself on the candidates. Talk with the elders of your church. Talk with your fellow members. Pray. Ask God for wisdom. And act.

—LONG VERSION—

It's tough to be honest when writing on the ethics of voting. You want to justify your voting patterns.

It might be even tougher to be *perceived* as honest. Readers naturally wonder, "Are you drawing those ethical boundaries in a way that favors your preferred candidate?" Call it a suspicion of ethical gerrymandering.

And it's a healthy suspicion. For you to wonder about me. For me to wonder about myself or anyone else on this topic.

CARELESS ARGUMENTS

A few years ago, at a dinner party of Christian academics, I sat next to a university professor who labelled herself politically liberal and pro-life. She said, "The Republicans are pro-life on abortion; the Democrats are pro-life on capital punishment. So I realized those two things cancel each other out, leaving me free to vote on other matters."

Leaving aside any feelings I might have about Democrats or Republicans, may I suggest that *this* sounded like gerrymandering ethics? She wanted to vote Democrat, so she mapped out a contorted argument to justify it. The thought bubble in my head read, "Wait, how many people have been put to death by capital punishment since the Supreme Court re-legalized it in 1976 *versus* how many unborn babies have been murdered since that time?"

I Googled this question when I got home. It turns out, as of January 2020, 1,512 people have been legally executed since 1976, when the Supreme Court re-legalized capital punishment. As of September 2020, the number of children murdered in the womb is more than 40,000x that: 62,061,402.

Even if you agree with her that the death penalty is in principle wrong—and even if you assume that every single one of those 1512 convictions was mistaken and that every one of those individuals was as innocent as the unborn children—consider the math: 1,500 does not equal 62 million. Not by a long shot. Those two numbers do not "cancel each other out."

I propose that this is a careless ethical argument.

DON'T DEFLECT, BE HONEST

All of us, of course, are susceptible to making careless, self-justifying ethical arguments.

Where I see this most clearly is in our deflections. For instance, when I correct one daughter for fighting with another, four times out of five the first words out of her mouth will be, "But she…" She deflects. And my reply is almost always: "I'll get to her. But right now I'm talking to you."

Likewise, if someone mentions an ethical challenge in voting for candidate "Jack" on Twitter, four of the first five replies will be, "But candidate 'Jill' is horrible!" To which I want to reply: we can talk about Jill, too, but are you willing to face head-on and square-shouldered the ethical challenges of voting for Jack?

Here's one way to know you're not being fully honest with yourself: you're unwilling to hear the moral challenges other people might offer of your preferred candidate, and you're unwilling to weigh and really wrestle with those challenges.

THE ETHICAL ASYMMETRY BETWEEN "YES" AND "NO"

Perhaps I can offer a hatch door to help you escape the temptation to deflect. First, you almost always have more than two choices when it comes to voting. Maybe you vote third party, write in a candidate, or just don't vote. A few counties have compulsory voting, like Brazil or Australia, yet even then they often have parliamentary systems with more than two choices, and there's always the possibility of civil disobedience. We'll reflect more on these possibilities in principle 7 below, but now I simply want to make the point that rare is the occasion that saying "no" to one candidate necessitates a "yes" to the other candidate.

Second, saying "no" to one path is ethically easier than saying "yes" to another path. There's a lower ethical bar. "You should" and "you should not" are not symmetrical. For instance, it's easier to tell a Christian woman she should not marry a certain non-Christian man than it is to say that she should marry a certain Christian man. Why? Because saying "no" is saying "no" to only one thing that's morally wrong, while saying "yes" is saying "no" to many things that may be permissible. More to the point, God doesn't give us the license to tell other people what positive course of action their obedience to God must take when they have multiple permissible options before them.

What all this means is, there may be times when a pastor or a Christian friend might reasonably say, "I don't believe you should walk down that path. In fact, I think it might be sin." Yet that's *not* the same thing as saying, "You must therefore walk down that other path." I'm

willing to say the former. I have a hard time imagining ever feeling the license to say the latter. And, frankly, it usually frustrates me when pastors do.

A BIT MORE CONTEXT

When I refer to the ethics of voting, I mean I'm interested in what makes a vote sinful or permissible. I'm not asking what makes a vote good or wise, which would require us to evaluate what the Bible says about the purpose of government and justice. I'm not going to tell you how to vote in this upcoming election. I'm not even going to tell you how to weigh all those principles listed below in order to yield the "most moral vote." I don't think that's possible in any of universal or systematic way. Two early readers of this piece reached the end and asked, "So what exactly are you saying?" I believe they were looking for a grand synthesis that they could then apply. I don't think I can offer that synthesis.

So what am I saying? I'm simply saying the nine principles below, all of which attempt to demonstrate how your vote is a moral activity—or an immoral one. That's all. And those nine principles then should help you to evaluate your own vote.

Further, as long as I'm still clearing my throat, I have struggled with knowing whether to articulate the principles below without showing at least a few of my personal convictions. On balance it seems more honest

and pedagogically useful to do both. I write as a Bible-believing Christian, and my political instincts tend to be conservative. Meaning, I believe there are moral challenges to voting in both directions, but you'll discern that I don't view those challenges symmetrically.

That said, I don't presume I'm offering the final or objective word. As Christians, we take our principles of right and wrong from Scripture, but thinking ethically about our vote always involves placing multiple issues on a balancing scale and making biblically unscripted judgments about how much they weigh in comparison to each other (e.g. see 1 Kings 3). The weight I give to all the rocks on the scale depends, at least in part, on my own life experience. And if there's one thing marriage has taught me, it's that my wife's experiences help me to weigh things a little differently.

If you don't share my conservative tendencies, hopefully you'll still find the principles useful. Yet you will bless the conversation by demonstrating what I've missed or how another set of experiences should cause me to weigh some issues differently. For instance, were I to spend several weeks trying to escape a war-torn country with children in tow and to cross a national border, I would probably weigh immigration issues a little differently.

Yet in all this, hopefully we can together take a step or two toward elevating the conversation which, in my estimation, is presently driven by carelessness and ideological tunnel-vision.

Lastly, I'm speaking out of the U.S. context, where the relationship between the voter and the candidate is slightly different than, say, in a European parliamentary system where party weighs more heavily. I'm confident others can better figure out how to apply it to their own electoral and political contexts than I can.

Here are nine principles on the ethics of voting, which build cumulatively. The first and the ninth may be the most crucial, with the third, fourth, and eighth a close second.

1. Your vote bears moral weight by virtue of a chain of causation.

When you vote in a democratic system, you are actually participating in the role of the "governing authorities" that Paul and Peter describe. Your job is to align your objectives with the purposes which God gives to the government in Scriptures, such as "punish[ing] those who do evil and praise[ing] those who do good" (1 Peter 2:13-14; see also, Gen. 9:5-6; Rom. 13:1-7; etc.).

Therefore, your vote requires you to make a moral evaluation about what's good and what's evil, or wise and unwise (see Prov. 8:15-16), and then to act on behalf of your evaluation. You are then morally responsible for this evaluation and act of judgment.

This is easy to see if we're talking about a ballot measure. In 2012, question 7 on the Maryland state ballot asked me and my fellow Marylanders "to increase from 15,000 to 16,500 the maximum number of video lottery terminals that may be operated in the State." A vote for or against that ballot measure was a moral decision by virtue of the moral significance of state lotteries. If I'm right, and state lotteries are unjust because they hurt the poor, then voting to expand commercial gaming by 1500 terminals is to participate in an injustice. And a person is morally culpable for that pro-lottery vote.

The moral significance of a vote is a little harder to see when talking about voting for a candidate, and I'm willing to say accountability decreases slightly due to a number of factors we'll get to. But a chain of moral accountability remains.

Suppose candidate Jack says he believes in positions *a*, *b*, *c*, *d*, and *e*, while candidate Jill supports issues *l*, *m*, *n*, *o*, and *p*. When I cast a ballot for Jack, I am giving Jack the *agency*—that is, the power or ability—he needs for turning *a*, *b*, *c*, *d*, and *e* into law over and against *l*, *m*, *n*, *o*, and *p*. If Jack is elected and succeeds in writing *a*, *b*, *c*, *d*, and *e* into law, I become morally culpable for those laws, at least in some measure.

I've found that people want to resist this. Sitting at lunch, one pastor friend responded, "Wait, are you saying I'm responsible for everything Jack says he's going to do?"

Basically, yes. To some extent. Other complexities will weigh in which, again, I'll get to. Still, we start right here with a basic chain of causality. Apart from our votes, Jack is just a solid-colored ball sitting in the middle of a pool table, shouting, "Send me to the side pocket!" But Jack is inert. He doesn't possess the agency or power necessary to get to that side pocket. Meanwhile, Jill is the striped ball, and she's campaigning, "Send me to the corner pocket!" But she, too, is stuck. Neither can move toward their desired pockets until the white cue ball of our votes rolls down the table, knocks into them, and gives them the agency they require to roll to their preferred pockets.

Which means, we possess a morally significant choice between Jack's side pocket (*a*, *b*, *c*, *d*, and *e*) and Jill's corner pocket (*l*, *m*, *n*, *o*, and *p*) because our votes create the necessary agency for one or the other. The transfer of moral culpability from Jack or Jill back to us is not as clean or scientifically exact as it is with a couple of inanimate pool balls on a smooth green table. The actions which candidates actually take once elected are unpredictable. They're human beings and will do things we don't anticipate. They'll also encounter circumstances outside of their control that prove far bumpier than the green cloth, including other balls rolling around the table trying to stop them from entering their intended pockets.

Still, insofar as a candidate promises and succeeds at reaching a certain pocket, moral responsibility travels back to us, the voters, who knowingly gave him or her the power to do so. It's the simple formula of cause and effect, and our vote is a first cause. It creates the requisite agency. We're handing Jack or Jill the sword of state.

So back to my pastor friend at lunch: "Are you saying I'm responsible for everything Jack says he's going to do?"

I replied, "If voting for Jack does *not* make me morally responsible for *a, b, c, d,* and *e* when Jack tells me that that's where he wants to go, then I'm not sure how my vote bears any moral weight whatsoever. It would seem voting is amoral. And my guess is that neither of us are ready to concede that."

2. With regard to what a vote *does,* your motives don't matter (but see point 8).

This point follows on the last one, and it's an even harder pill to swallow: your motives don't matter when you vote, at least in regard to what your vote *does.*

As I said, your vote gives a person agency. It hands him or her the sword of state. That's the real, undeniable, and concrete consequence of your freely chosen action, and you're morally responsible for it by virtue of this chain of causation. And in this regard your motives or intentions matter not a whit. Recall that Scripture does acknowledge a category for "unintentional sin" (Lev. 4).

You might hate Jack and his promise to pursue *a, b, c, d,* and *e,* but decide to vote for him as part of a long-term strategy, like a general ordering a strategic withdrawal today so that he can live to fight tomorrow. Still, you cannot discount what your vote *does.* It gives Jack agency to pursue *a, b, c, d,* and *e,* and you remain morally responsible for that.

You might believe issue *e* is wicked, yet vote for Jack because you really care about *a, b, c,* and *d.* Or because you think Jack's offering the lesser of two evils compared to Jane. Still, again, you cannot discount what your vote *does.* It gives Jack agency to pursue *a, b, c, d,* and *e,* and, again, you remain morally responsible for that.

Voting machines and ballots are dumb. They cannot discern any fine-tuned distinctions that might exist in our brains. Our votes are up or down. If you vote for Jack, you hand him the sword of state to pursue *e* just as much as you hand it to him for *a* through *d.* There's no way to absolve yourself of moral responsibility for the one thing you don't like and to keep it for the four things you do like.

You might even take other actions to undermine the bad effects of *e* while voting for Jack. Still, you cannot discount what your vote *does.* Other goods don't make that particular bad vanish.

To put it another way, which voters are morally responsible for Jack's pursuit of *e*? It has to be the ones who voted for him. Are just some of the people who voted for Jack responsible for his pursuit of *e,* or are all of them? It has to be all of them.

This is a tough pill to swallow, as I say, because few of us encounter candidates that agree with us on everything. Voting and party alignment always involves a series of pragmatic compromises. Still, we're morally culpable for those pragmatic compromises. When the Nazi soldiers pound on your front door and ask if you're hiding Jews in your basement, you might decide it's morally better to lie than to tell the truth and watch the Jews be carted away to concentration camps. Fine. I'd agree it is better. But the lie is still fraught with moral significance. You and I are making a moral wager that we hope will be vindicated in God's final assize.

Likewise, when you vote for Jack, you're taking on moral responsibility for *a, b, c, d,* and *e,* even if you hate *e.* And rather than deny this fact by appealing to your pious motives, you should accept it, square-shouldered, like a leader who's willing to accept responsibility for the good and bad of his or her decisions.

Professor of ethics Matthew Arbo has observed that, strictly speaking, we cannot cast a ballot against a candidate. The logic and mechanics of voting only allows us to say "yes" to someone. There's no way to say "no" to someone without also saying "yes." Of course, many people vote in order to say "no" to one side *in their minds or hearts*, but they can only do this by actually saying "yes" to the other side, as least from the perspective of the ballot. The problem is, that "yes" comes with moral baggage, say principles one and two. Our "yes" make us an accomplice with everything that candidate is promising.

3. There is a distinction between morally permissible laws and immoral laws which is crucial to our moral evaluations.

Some laws or actions promised by a candidate, in and of themselves, are morally permissible. In and of itself, it may be morally permissible to establish the tax rate at x percent, or to establish an immigration quota at y people per year, or to incarcerate a person for z years for possessing an illegal drug. Yet our moral evaluation of that tax rate, that immigration quota, or that sentencing standard might change over time as we watch the outcomes of these laws. We might discover a host of unintended injustices piling up that lead us to conclude that, in our time and place at least, an x percent tax rate, or y immigration quota, or z sentencing standard is effectively unjust.

In other words, the historical outcomes or consequences of otherwise morally permissible laws are relevant to our ongoing moral evaluation of those laws. If a morally permissible law produces an unintended, unfortunate outcome, like a welfare policy exacerbating cycles of poverty, or a sentencing standard leading to mass incarceration and the further destruction of families, a just response is to look for ways to alleviate that bad outcome, which may or may not involve changing the original law.

On the other hand, some laws, by their very nature, are always unjust (see Is. 10:1-2). So it is, for instance, with laws establishing race-based slavery, segregation, or discriminatory mortgage-lending practices. And so it is with laws establishing abortion.

Our posture toward morally permissible laws with bad outcomes should be different than our posture toward morally unjust laws. With morally permissible laws, we can talk about "reducing the bad outcomes," even while continuing to affirm the moral permissibility of a law. Not so with inherently unjust laws. The goal with unjust laws must be to overturn them, plain and simple, lest our ongoing support affirm what's inherently unjust. For instance, it would be inconsistent and perhaps even hypocritical to vote to "reduce the number of slaves" while also voting to uphold slavery laws. Again, the laws themselves are unjust.

Now, realpolitik considerations sometimes involve compromises. Half a loaf is better than no loaf, they say. For instance, I believe abortion is wrong from the moment of conception. Yet suppose I'm offered the chance to vote on a bill that changes the law from permitting abortion in all three trimesters to permitting it only in the first trimester. By voting for that law, I'm helping to ensure that fewer babies will be killed in the womb, and such a vote would seem to make good strategic sense, especially with a divided legislature that would never vote for overturning abortion entirely. But by accepting this compromise I'm also putting my hand to an unjust law. I'm saying "yes" to the profound injustice of killing babies in their first trimester. Is this the right thing to do, though, because of the preferred outcome—fewer babies killed?

I can see how Christians might arrive at different answers to that question. Yet my point here is to encourage all Christians to recognize the moral dilemma because "reducing the number of abortions" is categorically different than "reducing poverty" or "reducing automobile accidents." Abortion itself is intrinsically wicked in a way that tax rates and automobiles are not. So even if my temporary goal is to reduce the number of abortions, and I vote to outlaw abortion second and third trimesters even while affirming it in the first, my ultimate goal must remain overturning abortion entirely. I shouldn't be content stopping there.

4. The character of a candidate matters by the same chain of moral causation described in point 1.

Does the character of a candidate matter to the ethical significance of a vote? Yes, and it does by the same chain of moral causation described above, only now culpability transfers not through issues like *a, b, c, d,* and *e,* but through the person him or herself. If I choose a babysitter for my children whom I know has poor character, or a landlord for the apartment building I own whom I know has poor character, or a treasurer for my church whom I know has poor character, I become at least partially complicit in any bad decisions each of these individuals make.

Jesus tells us that, "Every good tree produces good fruit, but a bad tree produces bad fruit" (Matt. 7:17). If I knowingly plant a bad tree in my garden, is just the tree then responsible for the basket of bad fruit which my children carry inside? Am I not responsible, too?

The character of a candidate matters for at least three reasons:

(i) A person's character makes a candidate's promises more or less believable, which in turn makes democracy more or less workable and meaningful. It's true that we maintain veto power over dishonest candidates through our ability to kick the rascals out. Yet the moral and strategic value of a vote in any particular election depends on candidates striving to do what they promise to do. If Jill promises x but then pursues y, my original vote for her is meaningless for the length of that term of office. Democracy depends, in other words, on the honesty and integrity of candidates and office-holders.

Insofar as we vote for known deceivers, then, we become complicit both in their deceit as well as in any bad paths they choose—and we become complicit by the same chain of moral causation described in point 1 above. Ultimately, we become complicit in the weakening of democracy.

(ii) A person's character makes a candidate more or less trustworthy for making just decisions amidst the thousands of unpredictable decisions a politician makes while in office.

(iii) Perhaps most crucially, a leader's character and behavior teaches and even authorizes what's morally acceptable within that leader's domain. Suppose a baseball coach has a pattern of telling racist jokes. By doing so, he's teaching his players that racist jokes are acceptable. In a sense, he's even authorizing them to sit in the dugout and make such jokes among each other. Their consciences may tell them that other authorities (parents, league superintendent, etc.) would forbid such jokes. Yet their coach's actions, by virtue of his position, creates a little space in their consciences to do as he does.

So it is for leaders in every position. A police chief who looks the other way when his officers use excessive force implicitly authorizes the whole department to do the same, department policy notwithstanding. A pastor who gives himself to material acquisition teaches his church to follow.

The pattern of a leader's life—whether in the home, on the ballfield, in the c-suite, in the church, or in the nation—establishes the boundaries of acceptable behavior within his or her domain. People sometimes argue that a candidate's policy positions are more important than his or her character, and it's true that policies have an immediate and tangible effect on a body politic. Yet if a leader's character teaches, authorizes, and creates space for immoral activity, such as racism or deceit, then character, too, has a very real and tangible effect on a body politic that's analogous to passing a law. It's like the passing of an informal and unspoken law supporting those things, which people will notice and follow. Not surprisingly, therefore, Paul exhorted Timothy to watch his life and doctrine, saying he would save himself and his hearers by doing so (1 Tim. 4:16). A leader's life is powerful.

Suppose then you knowingly hire this baseball coach who makes racists jokes. Do you not risk becoming at least somewhat complicit in his racism? If so, might not the same principle apply to voting for a dishonest and unvirtuous candidate?

5. Saying "But Democracy!" doesn't sanctify your vote.

Just as our pragmatic compromises don't absolve us of moral responsibility for the concessions we make, nor does another argument I hear from friends: "But this is how democracy works. Surely there is always a morally righteous choice."

To which I say, maybe. Let's make sure we're not sacralizing democracy. I fear that our confidence in democracy tempts to believe we're absolved of moral responsibility for choosing the better of two compromised options.

But decision-making by "aggregative mechanisms"—as one of my political science professors described voting—is no guarantee of wholly holy choices. The precise mechanism and the constitutional structures behind it don't cover our decisions with a force-field of moral sanctity. Better to put on our grown-up pants and admit that acting in government involves making tough decisions, and that even the best decisions will entail

elements of the good, the bad, and the ugly. Just ask the general sending troops off to war. When we vote, we are participating in government decision-making, even if only in a limited respect.

To put this another way, receiving the opportunity to vote means stepping into the moral domain of power-holding, and with increased power comes increased moral responsibility. Westerners today treat the opportunity to vote fairly casually. We take it for granted as all-good. Yet we should take the moral stakes seriously, and recognize that sometimes there are no "clean" options for making tough leadership decisions.

I've never been a politician. But I am a pastor, and pastors regularly face this hard reality, particularly as they work through tough divorce, abuse, addiction, and other moral-crisis situations. Advise the broken family this way, and the wife suffers. Advise the family that way, and the kids suffer. Voting can be similar. Welcome to ethics in a fallen world.

6. There are a number of rocks on the scale, but some rocks are heavier than others.

Two principles are bound up in this point, and we need to pay attention to both simultaneously. On the one hand, a just government must attend to a multitude of issues—the economy, foreign policy, national defense, criminal justice, health care, various social issues, and more.

There are a number of rocks on the moral scales that Lady Justice must weigh. Victor Sholar rightly observes Christians shouldn't choose "between the immigrant or the orphan, the poor or the unborn, the police officer or the unarmed African-American." Therefore, a voter seeking to vote justly should always consider not just one or two issues but all the issues a candidate or party endorses, asking how much each one "weighs" morally.

On the other hand, some rocks are heavier than others (Matt. 23:23). They're more morally significant. Michael Sandel's trolley-car illustration from his book *Justice* captures this point. You are piloting a trolley car. You look down the tracks and see you are about to run over five people. There's not enough time to break. Yet right in front of the group is a rail split. You can grab the trolley handle and send it down a side track, but doing so will kill two people on that separate track. How much does it morally "weigh" to kill two people versus five? Most people would say it's better to kill two than five, but are you morally culpable for killing the two rather than the five because it involves your deliberate action rather than accepting what is otherwise an accident? Or what if the five were convicted murderers and the two are your spouse holding your child? Does this change your moral calculation? Either way, the illustration draws out the point.

Thinking ethically about voting means accounting for more than one rock, but it also means acknowledging that some rocks are heavier than others.

Or go back to the university professor I sat next to at the dinner party. She believed the moral weight of 62 million unborn children and 1500 convicted criminals can "cancel each other out." She rightly saw that there are multiple rocks on the scale. But I would say she wrongly did a poor job of discerning which rock was heavier.

The two principles raised here bring us to the matter of "one-issue voting." Some people say that one issue can outweigh every other issue, such that we can ignore the other rocks on the scale. Abolitionists in the 1850s felt this way about slavery. Pro-life advocates today believe this about abortion.

Perhaps a better way to justify one-issue voting comes from John Piper, who has observed the ethical asymmetry between what compels us to vote for a candidate and what might keep us from voting for a candidate. A candidate needs to be right on a number of issues to win our vote. Yet it might take only one issue to disqualify a candidate. Perhaps we want to support candidate Jack because he supports issues *a*, *b*, *c*, and *d*. But then we learn that Jack is pro-stealing, or pro-pedophilia, or pro-slavery. Most of us would say that that his stance on that one issue disqualifies

Jack. Piper then extends the argument to abortion. It should take more than a right stance on abortion to compel a Christian's vote (because there are a number of rocks on the scale). Yet the wrong stance on abortion should disqualify a candidate (because some rocks are heavier than others).

Of course, Piper's argument only works when the disqualifying issue in question divides the candidates. How would he have encouraged me to vote in the 2014 Maryland state election when the candidates for both major parties were pro-choice? Does that issue then cancel itself out, so that I'm free to vote on other issues, or should I count both candidates as disqualified?

Further, how do we weigh the deficiencies of a candidate's character on the scale with all the other rocks? Does Jack's bad character outweigh Jill's support of a wicked policy, or vice-a-versa? In fact, Piper believes that bad character can disqualify a person from the presidency just as much as support of a wicked policy. "I regard Donald Trump as not qualified for the presidency."

Whether one adopts Piper's argument that candidates can potentially disqualify themselves with one bad issue or through bad character—I do—hopefully every Christian recognizes the need to weigh out every rock on the scale as well as to give due consideration to which rocks may be heavier. Failing to pay

attention to both all the rocks and the heavier rocks makes us more susceptible to personal biases and gerrymandered ethics.

So here's a quick pastoral and confrontational word to you on this point, friend: our hearts see the biases of others far more quickly than their own, which is why Jesus warns us to start by searching for the plank in our own eyes (Matt. 7:3–5) and why he would not entrust himself to our judgments—"for he himself knew what was in man" (John 2:24–25). If you tell me that your judgment is generally impartial and unbiased, I'm going to accuse you, at best, of naivety and self-deception. One solution to our natural bent toward personal bias in weighing the different rocks is to recognize that people's different life experiences will enable them to better appreciate the weight of some rocks than you do. If I grew up with a single mom and attended failing public schools, or as a second-generation immigrant, or as one of nine children in a homeschooling Christian household, or as an ethnic minority, my life experience just might enable me to grasp the outcome or effects of certain policies in a way that others don't (see principle 3 above). Lady Justice needs to be blind-folded and impartial in one sense (see Ex. 23:3,6), yet in another sense she needs to make sure she really is weighing each rock properly by asking everyone to speak into an issue (see Prov. 18:17). My pastoral word, then, is: listen hard to people with different life experiences than your own—that you might weigh issues better, more objectively, more justly.

7. Is it morally permissible to not vote or to vote for a candidate that is certain to lose? It depends.

The challenges of weighing all those rocks leaves some people wondering if it's better not to vote at all. "If I vote for Jack, I'll effectively be condoning his terrible behavior and example. If I vote for Jill, I risk supporting her terrible support for issue *p*. Both directions feel like an endorsement of sin. Can I just stay home and not vote?"

Ordinarily, I believe it's morally better to vote than not to vote. God has given us a stewardship with the blessing of a vote, and we don't want to be like the servant who buried his talent in the ground. Why should we vote? For the sake of love of neighbor and justice. We love our neighbor by doing what we can to work for a more just government. If I'm driving the trolley car and I have a choice between killing two and five, doing nothing is killing five. And perhaps slightly better than killing five is killing two.

That said, I'm reluctant to make this an absolute principle. Loving neighbor and doing justice are absolute principles. But nowhere does the Bible say a person must pursue these things *by* voting. Plus, never

does an election hang merely on our decision, as in the trolley car illustration. Therefore, if a person is convinced in his conscience that he'd be sinning by voting for Jack and Jill both, I would say he shouldn't vote for either, so long as he is fully convinced in his mind. To borrow from the apostle Paul, "One person esteems one day as better than another, while another esteems all days alike. Each one should be fully convinced in his own mind" (Rom. 14:5).

Perhaps slightly better than abstaining from voting is to vote for a candidate that one's conscience can accept, even if that candidate is certain to lose. Those who vote for a losing candidate often anticipate the loss, even when the candidate belongs to one of the major parties. If your major party candidate is down in the pre-election polls by 10 percent, you still vote for him or her. The same dynamics apply when your candidate promises to only get a few votes: the rightness of your vote doesn't depend *merely* on possible outcomes, but on your faithfully affirming what is right. Even writing in a candidate, if one's ballot allows for it, is to participate in the election process and formally register what you believe is right and just.

8. With regard to church membership, your motives matter.

This point is particularly for Christians. It will take a little bit

of runway to get there, and if you don't like nuance in ethics, you won't like this point. Moral evaluation among Christians operates in two gears. Gear 1: our determination of right and wrong. Gear 2: our determination of wrongs that, apart from repentance, require excommunication or removal from membership in the church. What's key here is that not every moral evaluation in Gear 1 will downshift into Gear 2. It would be wrong for me to selfishly eat all the ice-cream in my house, and even to persist in a pattern of doing so. But my wife might understandably not raise my selfishness with our whole church. She would treat it as a sin with which to forbear.

The line between Gears 1 and 2 isn't always easy to discern, but most Christians would maintain that both gears exist because some sins are worse than others (e.g. Matt. 23:23) and because—frankly—it's not always clear what's a sin and what isn't. The lesser-of-two-evils illustrations above make the latter point. Is it a sin to lie about the Jews in your basement? Do either of the trolley car options involve sin? How will the Lord weigh such things on the Last Day? It's difficult to know.

Recognizing these two gears is useful because it allows us to face these tough ethical dilemmas and speak honestly to our own convictions while also creating some space for others to make different judgments.

I might be personally convicted that voting for candidate Jack is a sin because he supports state lotteries. Yet you're not convinced that lotteries are sinful, and so you vote for Jack. Driving in Gear 1, I would then say that you may be sinfully culpable for giving agency to Jack to promote state lotteries. Yet, having said that, I wouldn't then downshift my ethical evaluation into Gear 2 and say that I could no longer come to the Lord's Table with you. Why not? First, I recognize that I could be wrong about lotteries. Second, even if I'm right, not all sins rise to the level of significance that I would need to break fellowship with you.

Now, with all that set up, let's turn to the significance of motives for church membership with another illustration: voting for a pro-choice candidate. Unlike state lotteries, most Christians would affirm that abortion is wrong. We'd even use a word like *wicked*, meaning, the wrong is weighty. Furthermore, I would argue that voting for a pro-choice candidate, when other options are available, probably makes you sinfully culpable, according to principle 1 above. And I think this is true no matter what your motives are, according to principle 2 above.

But now let's think about your motives, supposing you share them with me. If you vote for a pro-choice candidate *specifically to support abortion*, I believe we shift from Gear 1 to Gear 2. Christians—I would

want to persuade my church—must not support abortion. They must not sponsor it, advocate for it, vote for it. And should someone in my church do so, I would recommend the breaking of Christian fellowship.

That said, suppose a Christian tells me she wants to vote for a pro-choice candidate not *because of* the candidate's support of abortion, but *in spite of* that support. She abhors the idea of abortion. At the same time, the idea of voting for the supposedly pro-life candidate makes her "want to throw up," as one Arabic Christian woman recently said to me. It would feel like voting for her own political self-destruction, she said, because the candidate "is against everything I am."

At this point, I believe five responses are simultaneously necessary. First, I would try to lean in with compassion, listen, and feel the weightiness of the rocks she's describing. That's especially important for someone like me who hasn't experienced what others have experienced, like this Arabic Christian woman. Scripture commands me to suffer with the parts of the body that suffer in 1 Corinthians 12:26, and the distinctions of that body—now look back at verse 13—include ethnic and political distinctions ("whether Jews or Gentiles, slave or free").

Second, while I would feel tempted in the moment to stop there and remove the ethical pressure of principles 1 and 2

above, I do feel consciously constrained to affirm my personal conviction that it would probably be sin for her to take the pro-choice path, and I would discourage her from taking it.

Third, I would exhort her not to do anything that would *defy her own conscience* before the Lord (Rom. 14:1–5, 22–23), such as voting for her own political self-destruction. My saying "no" to one path is not my insisting on "yes" to another path. Therefore, she should explore other options.

Fourth, I would affirm my willingness to come to the Lord's Table with her even if she finally disagrees with my judgment in this matter. I wouldn't break fellowship or recommend excommunication.

Fifth, leaning in a bit more, I would ask her whether she believed voting for the pro-life candidate was sin in light of all things that made her unable to vote for that candidate. If so, would she extend forbearance to members of the church who voted for that candidate?

The most difficult needle to thread in such a conversation is the fourth thing I just mentioned. If I'm personally convicted that her actions are probably sinful, why would I not recommend breaking of fellowship? The short answer is, her motives do make a difference to me, *at least in terms of how I would relate to her as fellow Christian.* And here the difference between *because of* and *in spite of* is meaningful. There's a strategic element to voting which we'll consider in the next point, and I recognize how a Christian might make different strategic judgments than me, even while I continue to maintain the basic wrongness of their position.

Does this mean Christians should accept any potential vote so long as the person says they're voting for a candidate *in spite of* the evil aims of the candidate? What if someone is voting for a member of the Ku Klux Klan or the Nazi Party? It's difficult to know how someone could vote for the KKK *in spite of* its racism and not *because of* its racism. The KKK exists expressly for the purpose of racism. So with Nazism. It existed expressly for the denial of God and the promotion of Arianism. No "because of/in spite of" divide seems possible. Supporting either of these parties would be more analogous to supporting an abortion provider like Planned Parenthood (regardless of how PP markets itself).

So, no, I'm not saying good motives allow us to maintain Christian fellowship with *any* vote a Christian might take. Yet if good motives are in fact conceivable, yes, we should be slow to break fellowship. However, when the occasion comes that a party exists almost exclusively for the purpose of wickedness, when a particular evil becomes an entity's *raison d'etre*, as with the Nazi Party or the KKK, then at that point

churches should consider excommunication for party membership or support. To be sure, there's no mathematically precise way to determine when that moment comes. It requires a wisdom-driven judgment call.

In short, Christians should be able to discuss voting with a moral vocabulary and as morally significant, and this means being willing to call some votes "sin." That said, the complex nature of the enterprise suggests we should leave space for fellow Christians to arrive at different conclusions without breaking fellowship. John Wesley believed the American colonists were disobeying God by rebelling from the British Crown. I hope he would have nonetheless accepted any revolutionaries in fellowship around the Table.

9. In the final analysis, ethically evaluating our votes involves *both* moral principles *and* strategic calculations.

Decision-making in politics in general and voting in particular is filled with tough moral calls, which is what principles 1 to 8 have highlighted. This is true not only because the issues are complex, but also because voting involves strategic calculations about how to get stuff done.

What does it mean for our moral evaluation to recognize the so-called "strategic realities" of voting? It means we need to view any given vote within the larger and highly elaborate *game* of

democratic governance. A game, of course, consists of several periods and many moves. Plus, you don't judge the success or failure of a game by any one period or move. You judge each move by how it contributes to the outcome of the whole game. Furthermore, your opponent's next moves are seldom predictable. Every decision is a calculated risk. Maybe you're convinced of one strategy, but you don't realize your opponent has prepared for it, and you'd be wise to consider another.

Likewise, principles 1 to 8 tell us we must pay attention to every distinct vote and ask what moral principles it affirms or denies. Yet principle 9 now reminds us that every particular vote is just one move or play in this larger game of governance. If the first principle above laid the foundation upon which the rest of the principles built, this last principle is the earthquake that shakes the building and makes the whole structure of our moral evaluation look a little less sturdy.

For instance, suppose a friend tells you he intends to vote for candidate Jack who supports something you both believe is wrong. Yet due to a host of realpolitik considerations, he believes voting for Jack is best for your shared cause in the long run. I have one friend, for instance, who believes the anti-Trump effect on state-legislates hurts the pro-life cause in state legislatures by turning them Democratic, as has arguably been the case in his own state legislature according to 2018 election exit-polls. Therefore, he's voting for Biden in the 2020 election, as he puts it, in order to help the pro-life cause in state legislatures. I'm not persuaded by his rationale. I think he's making all kinds of predictions about the future he should not make. Still, it's hypothetically possible he's right.

How then do we morally evaluate his action? His vote in 2020 is just one move in a larger multiyear "game." This brings us back to why the *because-of/in-spite-of* distinction is meaningful in terms of Christian fellowship. Nonetheless I find myself in an awkward situation: I believe he's probably sinning in his vote and I'll say so. But I'm not ready to break fellowship with him because he's seeking a good end, and it's hypothetically possible that in 10 years he will be proven strategically correct.

A similar dilemma faced many people who opposed slavery in antebellum United States. If someone in my church voted for a pro-slavery senator because he believed slavery was good and that African-Americans were less-than-human, then I would recommend we break fellowship with this member (assuming unrepentance). Yet suppose this fellow member sincerely lamented slavery, but believed that we need to slow-roll its abolition for the sake of preserving the union. Therefore, he was willing, nose between fingers, to vote for the pro-slavery senator, say, in the 1856 election because, by some calculated dynamic on the chess board of politics, he believed electing that senator versus the alternative would actually serve the cause of abolishing slavery in the long run. I'd *urge him* to do otherwise. I'd tell him that I believed he was sinning and that he would come to regret his vote. Yet it would be a little bit harder to recommend his excommunication. Ironically, the following decade would prove at least aspects of his political judgment accurate as the move against slavery really would tear the Union apart.

Yet notice what's crucial in my restraint from recommending excommunication: his goal must be to overturn an intrinsically unjust law, as in principle 3 above. He cannot wave off the injustice of slavery and say, "Well, it's never going to change. I might as well focus on other things." His heart would need to cry out against the injustice. A smidgeon of flexibility would be permitted only at the tactical level, not at the level of what his heart *and* actions must be set against.

Some will point to the strategic nature of voting and then effectively, if not explicitly, declare moral evaluation off limits. "How can you say their vote is 'wrong' if they're just adopting a different set of tactics?" For instance, why would I still call his pro-slavery vote sin, even if his judgment about the political realities would prove accurate? Because a Christian understanding of righteousness does not finally depend upon political realities, but on what's faithful and right, often in spite of those realities. "The body they may kill, God's truth abideth still."

Further, there's an element of "free-riding"—referring to the principle of economics—in such a decision to temporarily affirm what's evil for the sake of the longer path toward the good. If every Christian did on an ongoing basis what this imaginary anti-slavery voter who votes for the pro-slavery senator does, then the evil of slavery would never have been overcome. Slavery ended because enough citizens finally said, "Under no circumstances, no."

CONCLUSION

The moral complexity of voting tempts some people to give up on moral evaluation altogether, particularly in light of the strategic nature of the "game." My own sense is that it's better to affirm that our votes possess moral weight and then work hard at forming our convictions, which includes using the language of sin and righteousness. Yet we should also hold evaluations in this domain with a slightly looser grip.

The citizens of a democracy, including its Christian citizens, need to be able to make objective moral arguments and to do so with vigor, yet still leave some room for disagreement and the possibility that one might be in the electoral minority. Part of what makes room for disagreement possible, even as we use the language of sin and righteousness, is to acknowledge the limitations of our moral evaluations and strategic judgments.

I also believe that our moral evaluations should ordinarily quarantine themselves to the language of "should not" rather than "should." I recently read another writer's paper which laid out three categories of possibilities for the 2020 elections in the United States: Christians saying we should vote for Joe Biden; Christians saying we should vote for Donald Trump; and Christians saying we should leave every person to his or her own conscience.

For my part, I don't think we ordinarily possess the moral license to offer moral "shoulds" because there are almost always several permissible paths a Christian can walk. At most, from time to time, we might say "should not" to one path or another.

ABOUT THE AUTHOR
Jonathan Leeman is the Editorial Director at 9Marks.

4 Theological Principles for Christian Political Activism

Murray
Campbell

Engaging in political activism as a Christian is complex. As in many other topics, context matters. So let me explain myself. I'm an Australian pastor of a church in Melbourne, which is quite different than Manhattan, Memphis, or Miami. So some of my comments might need to be recalibrated for your context. If I were pastoring elsewhere, I assume I would have different emphases. But whether we're in the Great Southland or some other part of the globe, one thing is certain: conversations about religion and politics are fraught. Though I recognize the potential dangers, I do believe there's a place for Christian activism in the political sphere.

I want to offer four theological and pastoral suggestions for why and how Christians can be political activists.

1. BE CLEAR WHO YOU ARE SERVING: JESUS IS LORD OF ALL

"In his name the nations will put their hope" (Matt 12:21).

Jesus is Lord over creation and the church: "All things were made by him and for him." There's no domain over which he does not rule. In every home and every hall of power, Christ has ultimate jurisdiction:

> He was given authority, glory and sovereign power; all nations and peoples of every language worshipped him. His dominion is an everlasting dominion that will not pass away, and his kingdom is one that will never be destroyed. (Dan. 7:14)

Authoritarian secularism is on the rise in Australia, especially in my state of Victoria. Aussies have traditionally had a *laissez-faire* relationship with churches, respecting their role and voice in the public square, even if they often chose to ignore it. But over the past decade, this cordial relationship has been effectively dismantled. Churches were once politely acknowledged in society, but now Christianity is considered by many as a danger that needs to be silenced—or, at the very least, controlled. Unfortunately, Australia has few constitutional and legal protections for religious institutions. Religion has been pushed out of the public square, and on its way out there's been a growing agenda to increase governmental control over religious freedoms. This includes restricting what religious organizations may and may not teach on controversial issues, particularly marriage and human sexuality.

Should Christians, therefore, abandon the public square and remove themselves from the world of politics? I understand why many Christian *feel* like withdrawing, and there are fair arguments for doing so. But I want to contend that if Jesus is Lord over all, and if governments are put in place by God for the wellbeing of society, then at least some Christians should remain active in politics and societal engagement.

2. BE CLEAR ABOUT THE DOMAIN INTO WHICH YOU ARE SPEAKING: THE DISTINCTION BETWEEN CHURCH AND STATE

We should never confuse the state with the church or the kingdom of God. Too often, Christians mistakenly fuse Christianity with nationalism or the Christian message with a particular brand of politics; the results can be catastrophic.

At the same time, God tells us how the church should relate to the state. Churches are commanded to pray for the government (1 Tim. 2:1–2). This imperative isn't conditioned by our political preferences or by government decisions made in our favor. After all, Paul wrote at a time when there were no democratic societies and the government was largely intolerant of Christians.

Scripture also calls us to submit to and obey governing authorities, not because we agree with their policies but because God has put them in place (Rom. 13:1–6). Clearly, church and state, though separate domains, must relate to one another, even though the church recognizes the ultimate lordship of Christ over government authority.

For this reason, the church must not belong to, represent, or campaign for any political party. The church belongs only to the Lord Jesus Christ, not to the Liberal Party or the Labour Party (Australia's two major political parties). A Christian may choose to join a political party, but a church should not. Though once in a while a pastor might have to say, "No, a Christian cannot walk down that path," ordinarily the pulpit shouldn't be used bind consciences to vote along party lines. When a church does this, we confuse both Christians and non-Christians alike about our message and what it means to be a disciple of Jesus Christ. Instead of providing an alternative to our increasingly polarized world—instead of being the one place where true unity can be found and expressed—churches can end up reinforcing misconceptions about Christianity. Trying to squeeze Jesus under any socio-political umbrella is wrong; maybe he would prefer to stand out in the rain!

For example, at my own church, we never hand out political material, and we rarely promote petitions or marches. At the same time, we understand that individual Christians may choose to be involved in politics or promote social policies. While each member of the church supports and joins in the church's mission, believers have God-given opportunities to serve Christ in other ways outside the church: among these is involvement in political activity.

3. WHAT'S YOUR MESSAGE? UNDERSTANDING THE DISTINCTION BETWEEN GOSPEL AND COMMON GRACE

As an Australian citizen, I share the same set of rights and responsibilities as other Australians. I have the opportunity to voice concerns about social policy and moral issues. But not everything is the gospel, and not every political cause is directly related to the mission of the church.

Christians who are interested in engaging in the public square need to understand what the gospel is and isn't. They need to distinguish God's common grace from his saving grace. Defining social activism theologically provides us the necessary framework for understanding political concerns and weighing their importance. While there may be circumstances where a church renders judgment on a political matter, in most situations, such judgments are a matter of discernment for believers as they wisely apply biblical principles to political issues.

4. KNOW THE REASON FOR ENGAGING IN POLITICAL ACTIVISM: IT'S ABOUT LOVING YOUR NEIGHBOUR

For Christians, political activism ought to be about loving your neighbor. Just as a doctor treats the sick and a school teacher educates children, politics should be about serving the common good. Of all people, Christians have reason to speak on behalf of the vulnerable, to advocate for the weak, and to address injustices that are faced in our society. God has revealed his righteousness and his grace to us in the Lord Jesus. As he has loved us, so we now love others. We should be eager to see other people flourish. Not only should we care about their eternal salvation, but also about their everyday needs.

How do I know if my political advocacy is unwise and even ungodly?

Here are five warning signs:

- I spend more time signing petitions than I do praying.
- I only criticize one side of the political spectrum.
- People have the impression that belonging to my church means aligning with a certain political party.
- I'm more passionate about politics than I am about my local church and their mission.
- I'm putting my hope for society in political elections or leaders or platforms, rather than in the gospel of Christ.

"Therefore, as we have opportunity, let us do good to all people, especially to those who belong to the family of believers" (Galatians 6:10).

ABOUT THE AUTHOR

Murray Campbell is Lead Pastor of Mentone Baptist Church in Melbourne, Australia.

Pastoring Through a Contested Election: A Kenyan Perspective

Ken Mbugua

Since I'm about to talk about a topic as precious to us as politics, allow me to make a clarification as I begin. Contrary to popular opinion—perhaps even including that of the editors of this article—this is not *the* African perspective, nor is it *the* Kenyan perspective. In fact, what I'm about to say might not even be the perspective of the members of our congregation. I'm simply sharing one pastor's best efforts to lead his congregation through a season of political turmoil. So draw any counsel you might from the words below with caution. This is simply what Ken from Kenya thinks; Africa has not approved this message.

I'm yet to witness a Kenyan election that was not contested, save the General Elections of 2002 where we all got what we wanted: the ousting of the incumbent who had ruled for 24 years and the installment of a coalition government which we all believed would usher in the kingdom. Five years later, the elections were bitterly contested, and the country stratified yet again along tribal lines. Promises were broken, alliances were redrawn, and lives were lost. Beaming optimism devolved into bitter cynicism. The evil of our tribalism that we had managed to domesticate so well and for so long violently erupted into our society in all of its grotesque ugliness.

THIS IS US

Sadly, this affected our church.

Unkind, evil words were spoken with conviction by professing believers on both sides of the divide. Words were scrutinized, motives were judged, opinions were dichotomized, and the options were tyrannically simplified. Members displayed little empathy for one another.

So what did we do? We confessed our sins in our corporate prayer. We confessed not as tribalistic units but as united sinners who have been brought together through the blood of Jesus.

We also sought to interpret the state of our country primarily through our doctrine of sin. Our division as a nation was the surest evidence of our "division" from God. Our countrymen hated each other because they were haters of God. The nastiness in our national politics embarrassingly exposed our nastiness as humanity, reminding us that we're all self-destroying rebels who cannot fix ourselves. We need a Savior.

Even in the church, we need to remember this. We've not yet been totally purified of sin. We're still tempted toward everything that defined us before we came to Christ: *"evil, covetousness, malice. . . envy, murder, strife, deceit, maliciousness. . . gossips, slanderers, haters of God, insolent, haughty, boastful, inventors of evil, disobedient to parents, foolish, faithless, heartless, ruthless"* (Rom. 1:29–31). For these sins and many more we sought forgiveness from God.

If your aim is to be a faithful witness of God's truth in a season of political turmoil, then I suggest you start with a robust confession of sin. This strips us of any self-righteousness and self-pity that muddies our gospel witness to our communities. After all, the saints who see themselves primarily in the light of their well-studied political opinions are least likely to be the fragrance of God's truth to the onlooking world. We must remember that, apart from Christ, we would be miserable sinners. We ought to cry, as wretched men and women, "Who is sufficient for these things?"

POTENTIALLY PREJUDICED VS. GUILTY AS CHARGED

During this season of political unrest, it occurred to me that my voting choices were strangely aligned to my ethnicity. Do you know what else I noticed? The same was true for many of my friends, even though their particular voting choices were different than mine. All our votes closely aligned to our ethnicities even though each one of us would have argued that our tribal identity had little to do with our opinions.

I want to be clear: I hold my opinions because I believe them to be true. And yet, it's hard to say that I am entirely untainted by the tribal prejudices I have inherited not merely from Adam but also from my particular ethnic heritage. Without having to confess my political views as sin, I've found it useful to hold them with a healthy dose of suspicion.

As a pastor, this insight into my potential prejudices helped me hold to my political opinions with humility. That meant not sharing them broadly and avoiding arguments about politics in which I tried to convince others to cross over to my side of the divide. In short, I refrained from moralizing my political opinion. While some suggested it was sinful to celebrate the electoral victory of the president, others described the results as an answer to prayer and insensitively exhorted those who felt robbed and wronged to pray for the president "*as the Bible clearly instructs.*"

I and our church benefited because I didn't correct every perceived error nor did I engage every discussion. The complexity and intensity of politics can easily overshadow the unity that is ours in Christ. We can't let that happen. Instead, we must strive in the Spirit so that we display the gospel clearly to the glory of God. What did that look like in our church? Instead of intensity, we strove for gentleness. Instead of drawing lines and making demands, we strove for patience. Instead of making enemies with all who disagreed, we strove for bearing with one another in love.

LET BROTHERLY LOVE CONTINUE

After a bitterly contested election, it doesn't take a genius to know that some of your members will be angry and maybe even a little bitter. Meanwhile, others will be giddy and relieved. In our particular case, we had members who spent several nights huddled with their kids, frightened by the smell of teargas from the riots near their homes. We also had members who slept soundly. What did we do? We encouraged those who rejoiced at the result to abandon their rights for the sake of those who are not. We encouraged them to do a little more than spare a thought for those who were afraid. We encouraged them to actively serve them.

Pastoring through a contested election isn't like writing a position paper. It's attending to wounded sheep. It's calling members as brothers and sisters to check in on each other. It's opening up our homes for anyone who felt unsafe. It's fewer barbershop conversations about various theories related to politics and sociology and more empathetic interactions with a focus on the obvious needs around us. We don't need to agree on all the answers to show compassion, or to lament an obviously sad state of affairs.

And pastors, some people you've shepherded for years may call you an apostate because you mentioned the "J" word. Some may think you don't care about their pain because you pray about God's command to submit to the government. It's okay. In a time of turmoil, keep your primary focus on your sheep, and incessantly express compassion and love. This will go a long way.

PREACHING THE WORD

It was a fight not to get sucked into the categories society had established for us. When the political lines are drawn between "Justice" and "Peace," it's unlikely that believers will comfortably identify with either side of the divide. Though the heated conversations of the day sound all-important, we should remind ourselves that the Word of God endures forever. News channels, newspapers, and social media are filled with mere opinions. So, pastor, make sure you execute your God-given charge and preserve your pulpit for that Ancient Word. Don't confuse the value of any political insight with the value of God's Word for God's people.

In our case in 2017, the elder scheduled to preach on the Sunday after the controversial election preached from Obadiah. In that book, God had prepared a rebuke for many of us and an encouragement for all of us. Points in the passage weren't forced to fit into the political season. Instead, this brother faithfully preached the passage in front of him and allowed God to do the hacking and healing he wanted.

Just consider what Obadiah covers: God's justice, which had been directed to Judah in judgment, was now directed at the Edomites who "stood aloof on the day that strangers carried off the wealth of Judah." Those who gloated at the destruction of others were warned of God's coming judgment. And the sins God promised to judge went well beyond mere actions. He who sees all things will bring his righteous judgment upon their sinful attitudes toward their "enemies." What's more, God announced that all nations would face his impending judgment. Meanwhile, Obadiah offered the hope of God's coming kingdom.

If there's ever a time to trust in the sufficiency of God's Word, it's in the midst of political turmoil. When your people look to you and ask what "word" you have for them, make sure that you aspire for nothing more than being a faithful herald of God's Word both in season and out of season. Faithful preaching in a season of political turmoil will offend and encourage indiscriminately. It will reshape the boundaries politics has erected and promote a peculiar unity not around shared political viewpoints but around deeper, more enduring truths. Faithful preaching will lead you and your people to regular repentance and reified faith in our crucified, raised, and ascended King, the One who is indeed coming soon.

ABOUT THE AUTHOR

Ken Mbugua is a pastor of Emmanuel Baptist Church in Nairobi, Kenya.

Pastoring in Political Turmoil

Marwan
Aboul-Zelof

My family and I moved to Lebanon four years ago with the hope of planting a church in Beirut. By God's grace, we planted City Bible Church in the spring of 2018.

Lebanon is a spectacular country with a rich history. Her beauty is even recorded in the Bible. But for several thousand years, she has been plagued with destruction and corruption.

Two weeks after we moved to Beirut, a new president was voted in, effectively ending a two-and-a-half-year stalemate in the country. An incredible sense of hope and pride filled the country. That feeling is all but gone.

In my time here, I've noticed how the tense and fragile political climate has directly affected Lebanon's citizens and residents. During the Syrian refugee crisis, Lebanon had more refugees per capita than any other country in the world (one-in-four people were refugees). The country has been on the brink of war several times. Currently, Lebanon is experiencing an economic crisis unlike anything in her modern history.

Recent reports indicate that Lebanon is the first country in the MENA region to see its inflation rate exceed 50% for 30 consecutive days. The years of political corruption and lack of financial accountability since the Lebanese Civil War (1975–1990) has practically made Lebanon a failed state.

After months of increased prices on basic goods and the introduction of new taxes, Lebanese people hit the streets in protest. What's now known as the Lebanese Revolution started on October 17, 2019. The majority of Lebanese people are calling for all the politicians to step down, and for a new government system to be established. Incredibly, the government has resigned twice since the start of the revolution. The first time was shortly after the revolution began; the second came a week after the Beirut explosion, the same one that blew up our church building.

The revolution has also deepened the difficult economic situation, though it's in no way the cause of its current woes. The COVID-19 pandemic has crippled the economy even more than we previously experienced. And we've yet to see the effects that will follow the recent explosion and our now-empty parliament.

So, what does a young pastor in a new church plant do in a time like this? How much should a pastor speak into the political turmoil? Am I responsible to address the corruption that our church sees in every area of Lebanese life?

I certainly have more questions than I do answers. But I've found a few biblical principles that help me navigate and shepherd in these politically turbulent times.

1. PREACH THE BIBLE.

God's Word is living and active. It is powerful to save from sin and to break any bondage that's found in this world.

As ministers of the gospel, our duty and joy is to faithfully serve our church the eternal truths of Scripture. I know there's a temptation to use our pulpits as a platform to address the issues of the week. But our people need the wisdom of God to endure such confusing times.

I've experienced such freedom and boldness to stand upon God's Word, especially in these turbulent times. His Word has been an anchor to our congregation. He has been faithful to address not only our greatest need, but our present needs as well. I trust that the Holy Spirit will speak to his people through his Word, and this is the hope I hold onto every time I stand behind the pulpit.

2. LISTEN TO YOUR SHEEP.

So many voices and streams of information are available to us now that we sometimes think that we're ready to speak to the church without ever taking time to listen to their actual concerns. Pastors, remember that what you see and read on social media often isn't the reality and experience of your church members.

Taking time to listen to our members, especially on issues surrounding Lebanese politics, has greatly helped me shepherd the flock. I've found that I can bring these questions up during pastoral visits and in discipling conversations. Pastors must remember to listen to the voice of those God has given them to shepherd.

3. HIGHLIGHT OUR SHARED IDENTITY IN CHRIST.

Our union with Christ is the most important thing about us, even though we still struggle with the temptation to find our worth in other places. We desperately need to be reminded that, first and foremost, we're those who have been saved by grace through faith. Any other ways we identify ourselves must fade to its proper place.

Diversity within the church is a gift from God. Of course Christians are ordinarily free to identify with a certain political party, or recognize themselves as part of a nationality or ethnic group. But our identity and union with Christ is greater than any other allegiance; it must override all others.

Pastors must declare this truth regularly because we're often pressured to identify ourselves with something other than Christ. This is certainly the case in Lebanon. Every citizen's personal record reflects their family religion, their patriarch's hometown, and their political party (which is based on their religious identity). Where I live, family names and tribal alliances aren't a thing of the past.

A clear understanding of our identity in Christ must shape how we interact with one another in the church. It should allow for both the grace and the space to dialogue with those who hold different social or political views.

4. URGE PEOPLE TO HOPE IN GOD.

Though we know we should only set our hope in God, we're still drawn to lesser saviors. In times of national elections and political turmoil, we need to keep our hope directed toward Christ.

Simply put, Christians must live differently than those in the world. Our hope must never be placed in a party, a politician, or a system of government. Our people need to be reminded to hope in God alone. We must teach them not to get swept up with the ambitious promises that come with every political season. Political dreams will fail, and if our people aren't properly taught, those failed dreams will drive them to despair. We must hope in eternity because our citizenship is not of this world.

5. REMIND THEM OF THE SOVEREIGNTY OF GOD.

The sovereignty of God is a source of assurance and hope in this broken world. When chaos and corruption abound, few truths are sweeter than "God is in control."

Of course, trusting God's sovereignty doesn't take away the challenges of political turmoil. It's difficult to understand why God would place certain earthly authorities in positions of power. In the midst of a revolution, it's challenging to know how to lead the church to submit to the authorities placed over us when they are so evidently corrupt and wicked.

For instance, the recent Beirut explosion, which destroyed our building, was the result of gross negligence on the part of the government, even if it did happen by accident. The government had allowed dangerous materials to be stored near the middle of the city for years. As a result, thousands of homes and businesses have been destroyed. Over 220 people have died, thousands are injured, and hundreds of thousands are experiencing damage, loss, and trauma. Knowing that God is sovereign is our only peace in the midst of such destruction and brokenness.

There may be times when conscience and conviction won't allow a person to submit to earthly authorities. And yet, as those who believe in God's sovereignty, we know that in every way we submit here on earth we are ultimately submitting ourselves to God. If nothing else, this posture reminds us of our need for God. We must trust that all his providences are for his glory and our good.

6. SPEAK TRUTH AGAINST SIN.

Just as wars, sickness, and death show creation's brokenness, contested elections, revolutions, and political turmoil do the same.

Pastors must speak against injustice and corruption because the church is founded on and committed to uphold truth. If we avoid calling out sin in social or cultural matters, then what right do we have to speak of sin in the lives of our flock? Surely, some political matters are unclear, and Scripture may not speak directly to it. But when sin is clear, and the opportunity is available, pastors are obliged to speak against it.

Anytime we discuss sin, we have a wonderful opportunity to declare the power of the gospel. Our church needs to hear each week that the gospel is able to save even the most corrupt and wicked politician. Our people need to be reminded that sin is our great enemy, and that in Jesus we have a great Savior.

Ultimately, pastoring our churches through political turmoil isn't much different from pastoring them in any other season of life. Our sheep need to know that they are broken and that this world is broken. They need us to point them to Jesus. They need to repeatedly hear from God's Word that our only hope, both in life and death, is that we are not our own but belong to God.

ABOUT THE AUTHOR

Marwan Aboul-Zelof is the planting pastor of City Bible Church in Beirut, Lebanon

Pastoring Undocumented Workers in Civil Unrest

Alejandro
Molero

Several years ago, I left Venezuela to plant a Spanish-speaking church in Washington, DC.

If you've read international news in the last 10 years, you're likely aware that I left behind a deeply complex web of socio-economic crises and political struggles. I pastored a church in Venezuela for 14 years in my hometown. We faced intermittent seasons of political riots, marches, and protests. People in my city were often unable to find food and medicine; safety was an everyday concern. Even though I miss my home country and the church I pastored there, I admit I felt some measure of relief when I landed at Reagan National airport.

Yet here I am again: different country, similar protests; different reasons, similar chaos spilling onto the streets; different slangs and slurs, same hate-filled hearts.

A few weeks ago, just a few blocks from my house, I smelled an old, familiar smell: tear gas. And upon seeing wood panels covering storefronts all over the city, I feel an old, familiar feeling: sadness and despair in the public square. Worst of all, there seems to be no light at the end of the tunnel as both the problem and their solutions are being co-opted for political purposes. As it turns out, my new home is starting to feel a lot like my old one.

I don't pretend to be an experienced revolution survivor, much less a social scientist. I'm a pastor—a servant to the largest non-American minority in the heart of this nation's capital. Most Hispanics have come here with a singular purpose: to make money. They've been mistreated for decades by discrimination and marginalization. Now, in a nation-wide confrontation over racism that has been exasperated by an ominously long pandemic, the people I serve are struggling to find affordable food, steady jobs, prescription medication, and trustworthy immigration processes.

Looking at the neighborhood around me, I serve a population with several fears. Many of these folks are either illegal or undocumented. Christians and pastors have different responses to America's immigration challenges. I won't address all the ethical and legal complexities here, but our church's location gives us plenty of opportunity to think about loving and sharing the gospel with these folks.

The workers in our community are underpaid. Many need to work 60+ hours per week in order to care for their families. They don't have health insurance, drivers' licenses, or even bank accounts. They struggle through language barriers. Some of them face xenophobic assaults or episodes of discrimination they cannot report to any authority. Most of them are concerned about being deported. On top of that, businesses continue to shut down and opportunities for work are becoming increasingly rare.

In the midst of all this, our church has sought to help

provide our neighbors with food for their bodies and peace for their souls. In the last 20 weeks, with the help of sister churches, we've assisted 576 different families. Based on James 2:15–16, we've prayed with them, shared the gospel, filled their bellies, and paid some of their bills. Hopefully, they know we love them. Not all of them will come to Christ, but we're sowing seed and trusting the Lord of the harvest. We're encouraged.

But we're also sad. Over the last 20 weeks, we've had several heartbreaking conversations with people in our neighborhood:

- JD, a Colombian man, came to my house early one morning because he had an appointment to sign divorce papers. He feared that he was going to be deported immediately: "Pastor, I have nobody else. If I get deported, I want you to keep of my few belongings in this briefcase: my passport, my clothes, my wallet, and my most precious thing—an iPad with a lot of pictures of my little daughter. You're the only one I can trust. Here's some cash to mail me this briefcase when I call you from Colombia".
- DG, a Guatemalan woman, told us that her husband beat her for years. When she finally decided to run away, she went to the police and asked for a restraining order. But one day he tracked her down and beat her severely. When her husband was finally put in prison she told me, "If my husband kills me when he gets out of prison, I want you to take care of my daughter. Please, receive her in your home. You are the only ones I can trust." That broke our hearts in a thousand pieces.
- MM, a Costa Rican woman who left her family two years ago and overstayed her lawful tourist visa, was devastated when she discovered that her 21-year-old daughter died in a car accident last October. She couldn't make it home to attend the funeral. After losing her job, she was on the brink of homelessness. Hungry and impoverished, she stood outside a food bank for several hours waiting for a box of groceries. Before she got them, the program was shut down for not complying with social distancing rules. Despairing, she cried out loud to heaven, Why so much humiliation, Lord? What else shall I go through? In that moment, somebody else in the line gave her the contact information for our church. She called us, and we were able to buy her groceries. I prayed for her, and she prayed a touching prayer of faith asking the Lord for mercy. Since that memorable moment, she has consistently joined our online church meetings twice a week with great joy in the Lord.

In all these cases and in many more, we trust the risen and ruling King Jesus to draw many to himself as we imitate his grace and kindness in shepherding undocumented workers amid civil unrest. "Only, they asked us **to** remember the **poor**, the very thing I was **eager to do**" (Gal. 2:10).

If your church is surrounded by undocumented workers, what can you and your congregation do to love them? At some point you will need to discuss what it means to obey the government. In the meantime, maybe think of them as something like the Samaritans of our day, the class of people the establishment despises and ignores. Will you share the gospel with them, even as Christ did? Will you show hospitality?

And so we pray: Come Lord, Jesus!

ABOUT THE AUTHOR

Alejandro Molero is the pastor of Iglesia Bíblica Sublime Gracia in Washington, DC.

Other Resources

SMALL GROUP STUDY GUIDE: THE BIBLE AND POLITICS
https://www.9marks.org/wp-content/uploads/2018/04/HowNatRage_10dayDevo_v02.pdf

SUNDAY SCHOOL CLASS MANUSCRIPT: CHRISTIANS AND GOVERNMENT
https://www.9marks.org/article/what-christians-should-do-for-government-love-your-nation-people-or-tribe/

BOOKS ON FAITH AND POLITICS BY 9MARKS AUTHORS:
- God and Politics
  https://www.amazon.com/God-Politics-Mark-Dever/dp/1910587435

- How the Nations Rage: Rethinking Faith and Politics for a Divided Age
  https://9marks.myshopify.com/products/how-the-nations-rage

- How Can I Love Church Members with Different Politics?
  https://9marks.myshopify.com/products/how-can-i-love-church-members-with-different-politics

TGC ARTICLE: THE RELATIONSHIP OF CHURCH AND STATE, BY JONATHAN LEEMAN
https://www.thegospelcoalition.org/essay/the-relationship-of-church-and-state/